TEE exemplifies a model of th[ ] missional in its purpose and d [ ] equips disciples and empowers churches to serve God's mission in the world. This book not only explains the TEE philosophy and methodology but also demonstrates the impact of TEE training on learners, their churches, and their communities through the testimonies it contains. What an encouragement it is to read stories of the rapid growth of churches, especially in the difficult places, through TEE groups. TEE is definitely a gift to us in Asia!

Theresa Roco-Lua, EdD
General Secretary, Asia Theological Association

We live in exciting times, with unprecedented growth of the church across Asia. The need for quality leadership calls for approaches that not only provide solid biblical training but also holistic development. *TEE in Asia: Empowering Churches, Equipping Disciples* presents us with both theological and theoretical foundations for quality, church-based training with practical examples and stories that bring to life what God is doing in the region through the ministry of TEE. A must read for anyone serious about furthering a strong and growing church in Asia and beyond.

Perry Shaw, EdD
Former Professor of Education,
Arab Baptist Theological Seminary, Beirut, Lebanon
Author of *Transforming Theological Education*

I wholeheartedly endorse this much-needed book. It is easy to read, accurate, and has a useful reference bibliography. The book gives a basic but comprehensive understanding of how TEE works. But more importantly, it shares the thrilling results through personal testimonies of how the lives of thousands of individuals and churches have been transformed and empowered by studying and living God's word through TEE. My hope and prayer is that this book will inspire many more churches to consider and use Tools to Equip and Empower in their ministries.

Rev Terrick J. Barratt
International Director, Study by Extension for All Nations (SEAN)

ICETE Series

TEE in Asia

ICETE International Council for Evangelical Theological Education
strengthening evangelical theological education through international cooperation

Langham
GLOBAL LIBRARY

TEE in Asia

Empowering Churches, Equipping Disciples

Edited by

Hanna-Ruth van Wingerden
Tim Green
Graham Aylett

Series Editors

Riad Kassis and Michael A. Ortiz

ICETE International Council for Evangelical Theological Education
strengthening evangelical theological education through international cooperation

Langham

GLOBAL LIBRARY

© 2021 Increase Association

Published 2021 by Langham Global Library
An imprint of Langham Publishing
www.langhampublishing.org

Langham Publishing and its imprints are a ministry of Langham Partnership

Langham Partnership
PO Box 296, Carlisle, Cumbria, CA3 9WZ, UK
www.langham.org

Previously published as a private publication by the Increase Association in 2018, under the auspices of the Increase Trust UK, in the UK. Statistics and data in this book were accurate in 2018.

ISBNs:
978-1-83973-065-8 Print
978-1-83973-089-4 ePub
978-1-83973-090-0 Mobi
978-1-83973-091-7 PDF

British Library Cataloguing-in-Publication Data
A catalogue record for this book is available from the British Library.

ISBN: 978-1-83973-065-8

Cover & Book Design: projectluz.com

We dedicate this book to the thousands of TEE group leaders all across Asia who are investing their time, their lives, and their hearts to disciple believers for the glory of God.

Contents

Foreword

A s I open this book, I see the faces and hear the voices of many thousands of TEE students from different countries of Asia and beyond, and I reflect on the testimonies of their changed lives, their stories of miracles and victories over sin, and their new directions for ministry as a result of their studies. Is there a bigger miracle than the changed life of one person? If a changed life is a miracle, TEE has a miraculous history because God has used it to change the lives of many Christians – and he continues to do so in amazing ways and to prepare multitudes of God's servants for ministry.

TEE (Theological Education by Extension) started in 1960s, was popular in 1980s and 1990s, and in our days experiences a true revival spreading quickly to new countries and churches. Since the beginning of this century, the most significant changes in TEE have taken place in Asia and the adjacent regions where Christians are often a religious minority living in a hostile environment and often experience persecution and economic hardship.

The people who prepared this book have a real passion for TEE, and you will feel this passion as you read this book. The book briefly and clearly explains TEE history and methodology and presents a picture of TEE in different countries of Asia today which are illustrated by many true stories. The book also shows the important new trends in TEE: the birth of national TEE teams in new countries, the growth of partnership between TEE teams, the improvement of group leader training, the creation of new courses relevant for the modern church, the growing interest in TEE from higher residential institutions, the use of new technologies, and the spread of TEE among diaspora churches. The book also contains an extensive bibliography of works on TEE published since 2000.

TEE in Asia reflects the serving role which the Increase Association plays in bringing the TEE forces together and providing a platform for the improvement and partnership of national TEE teams in different countries by organizing conferences and workshops, helping the teams to be connected, and raising awareness of TEE in the global community.

As a TEE practitioner and one of the pioneers of TEE in the post-Soviet countries, I am totally convinced of the significant value of TEE for the churches in that big region, its growing recognition among churches of different denominations, and its impact on the lives of Christians. However, TEE strengthens not just individual believers but whole church fellowships. It empowers churches and equips disciples. It represents a true movement of God and is his instrument for the discipleship of multitudes in the end times when the church is being tested by the pressures of growing persecution and false teachings. TEE fills the minds of God's people with the knowledge of his word, sets their hearts on fire for God, and prepares them for the mission of God on this earth. It also breaks denominational barriers and brings more unity to the church.

In our days, TEE has become one of the most successful and effective forms of church-based theological education which is affordable and suitable for Christians of different nationalities, denominations, educational backgrounds, age, gender, and life and job situations. However, to become and remain even more successful and effective requires the combined effort of TEE experts, residential institutions, denominational leaders, prayer partners, and donor organizations.

I would like to thank the authors of this book for the immense work they have done to present this detailed and inspiring picture of modern TEE developments in Asia and beyond.

Anneta Vysotskaya
Increase Association Committee Chair

Preface

About Increase

Increase is an association of church-based training organizations rooted in and around Asia – from Egypt to Indonesia and most places in between, as well as in far-flung diaspora. Increase member movements are helping churches in their own countries to make disciples and grow their own leaders. This work is led not by expatriates but by national believers pioneering new initiatives for their own people. Increase members unite around this big vision: *Churches equipping all Christ's followers in their context, so that many millions are discipled and empowered for mission, ministry, and leadership.*

Increase member movements mostly use a training method called TEE. Traditionally, this stands for Theological Education by Extension. But in today's world it is more easily understood as Tools to Equip and Empower: tools for local churches to equip and empower all their members to grow in Christ and serve him actively.

- Section A of this book explains how TEE works.
- Section B tells the stories of how churches are using TEE to equip about 100,000 Asian Christians week by week in their local contexts.
- Section C explains how Increase is helping to bring innovation in twenty-first century TEE.

When people in the West pray for Christians in Asia, they may think only of "those poor persecuted believers." Yes, believers in some Asian countries suffer for their faith, but also many churches are tenacious, bold, and growing vigorously. They have much to teach the West. Read on to see what God is doing across the region through today's TEE movement. Be thrilled. And find out how you might join in.

Rev Dr Tim Green
General Secretary, The Increase Association

To the Reader

From Us . . .

This book is truly a joint effort. So many people have been involved! Not just the three editors on the front cover, but countless others from many countries, including the contributors listed on the previous page. Many chapters were written in close partnership, and even the chapters written by a single person could not have been finished if not for the input, feedback, and advice of others.

All the national teams you will read about had the chance to read, comment on, and correct the chapters that introduce them. The book in your hands is only possible because of their input, and they provided us with the information and the testimonies. The individuals featured in the short stories are all happy to share their personal journey of faith with you.

We have tried to be reasonably consistent in our use of language throughout this book. However, we wanted to take into account the cultural differences that exist throughout Asia. Some people say things differently than others, and we have tried our best to respect that. An example is mentioning titles (e.g. Rev, Dr, and so on) in some of the chapters. Many cultures see the use of titles as a sign of respect: they value this use, and we have tried to honour their values.

. . . To You

This book will help you to pray for and connect with the people that shape TEE in Asia today. When you read people's testimonies, you will understand that there are many things you could be praying about! But to help you, we've also included a few concise prayer needs at the end of each chapter.

But there's more. You can also get in touch with these teams! Most have included contact details so you can ask them how you can get involved. Is there something you would like to know more about? Do you want to encourage teams? Use this opportunity to connect with them!

If you want to start using TEE courses in your church, the Increase Association or the team in your country can give you more information on how to do so. If you feel like you want to get involved in the ministry, join a course writing team, or work with a national team, this book gives you opportunities to do so. Have a look at the "Suggested Next Steps for You" section in chapter 35 for inspiration. So don't wait any longer. Read, pray, and connect!

Acknowledgements

This book would not exist without the efforts of many people who devoted their time, attention, creativity, and wisdom to it. Without their input, it would not have been possible. We are so grateful to all the people, named or unnamed in this book, who have given their testimonies and shared with us how God is transforming their hearts, their communities, and their country.

We thank Claire Boxall, Penny Vinden, and ML Low for their time given to interviewing people at the Increase conference "Empowering Churches, Equipping Disciples" in November 2017. They also wrote some chapters or parts of chapters, and David Ball and Bob Teoh wrote others.

Chen Yoke Mee made our lives a lot easier by transcribing the many video testimonies and conference presentations. Thank you! A huge thank you goes to Ee Chong Kok of Art Printing Works Sdn Bhd.

We are grateful to all the people who read draft chapters and checked for spelling and style. Thanks especially to Dorothy McMillan, Michael and Pauline Huggins, Gloria Dean, Mike Butterworth, and Pieter van Wingerden. Thank you also to Pieter for formatting the bibliography so carefully! Thank you to Terry Barratt, David Ball, and Patricia Harrison for your time and helpful advice in shaping some of the chapters.

Thank you so much to all the leaders and team members of the Increase member programs for helping us to make this book a lot better. Your feedback and input mean such a lot to us! This book is about you, and it has been an honour to write about your work.

Thank you ML and Monica for your creativity and hard work on the design and photography of this book. Rachel Green, we really appreciate your time in sorting through the huge piles of available photos and proofreading the whole book alongside Yoke Mee!

Thank you Dr Theresa Lua, Dr Perry Shaw, and Rev Terry Barratt for taking time to read the draft of this book and write your commendations for it.

It would not have been possible to finish this book without the people who supported the project, and us personally, in prayer. Hanna-Ruth wants to thank

Fenna Brouwer and Maaike Heringa for their ongoing prayers. Thank you to Jolyon Trickey for mobilizing prayer through the Increase prayer updates and the Intercessors team. Thank you to all those who prayed through the process of bringing this book to birth!

There would be no book about TEE in Asia without our Lord Jesus Christ who uses these ordinary materials and all these ordinary people in extraordinary ways to bless and grow his church. Lord, we are amazed at what you are doing. Thank you!

Abbreviations

ATA	Asia Theological Association
C&MA	Christian and Missionary Alliance
CAMACOP	Christian and Missionary Alliance Churches of the Philippines
CCTB	College of Christian Theology Bangladesh
CLD	Center for Leadership Development
CLTC	Christian Leaders' Training College
CLTEE	Community Learning TEE Indonesia
EBC	Evangelical Brotherhood Church
GKJTU	Gereja Kristen Jawa Tengah Utara
ICETE	International Council for Evangelical Theological Education
IFES	International Fellowship of Evangelical Students
ITEEN	Institute of Theological Education by Extension Nepal
ITEEP	Institute for Theological Education by Extension, Philippines
KEC	Khmer Evangelical Church
KLTC	Kingdom Leadership Training Center
KTEE	Korea TEE Ministries
MBTS	Malaysia Baptist Theological Seminary
MSP	Hmong Ministerial Study Program
ORTA	[The TEE team in Russia]
OTS	Open Theological Seminary
PTEE	Program for Theological Education by Extension
SEAN	Study by Extension for All Nations
SKT	Shikkha Kalyan Trust
TAFTEE	Association for Theological Education by Extension
TEE	Theological Education by Extension or Tools to Equip and Empower
TEEAC	TEE Association of Cambodia
TEECL	TEE Community Learning, Korea
TMCC	TEE Movers for the Chinese Church
WEA	World Evangelical Association

Part A

Explaining TEE

© ML Low

1

God's Mission and Ours

Penelope Vinden and Graham Aylett

From Genesis to Revelation there is a great theme: God is on a mission! In history and in story, through poetry, letter, and prophecy, in wonderful varied ways God reaches out to humanity, bridging the great chasm caused by sin.

God is on a mission to totally restore his creation to all that it is meant to be. That means everything – animals, plants, the oceans, and the atmosphere – but above all humankind, created in his image. Paul speaks in Romans chapter 8 of creation groaning while it waits for its liberation and the redemption of God's people.[1] We too as Christians await the fullness of our redemption.

God's mission to redeem unfolds in a glorious new way in the sending of his Son to earth. The New Testament looks forward to the day when everyone everywhere recognizes Jesus as Lord, when everything that stands in the way of God's rule is removed, when all the nations are singing the praises of God, and when all creation is set free from decay and death.

That God wants to do all of this is one of the amazing mysteries of our faith. That he does not abandon the world and its people to the chaos of our willful rebellion against him is astounding. But perhaps an even greater mystery is that he calls us to be part of that great restoration. God is on a mission, and we are part of it.

---

1. Romans 8:19–23.

Our Part

To use us in his mission, God must forge a people, his church, who display his character. Is he holy? We are to be holy. Is he just? We must be just. Is he faithful, compassionate, merciful? His church must be, too. God is building a people who are passionate about the things that matter to him, who are moved by the things that move him. He wants his church to share in his big plans for his creation. His mission is our mission.

What is our mission? It is simply seeing what God is doing and joining in. Old Testament scholar Chris Wright puts it this way: "Mission is not ours; mission is God's. Certainly, the mission of God is the prior reality out of which flows any mission that we get involved in. . . . Mission was not made for the church; the church was made for mission – God's mission."[2]

Equipping All of God's People for God's Mission

If all mission is God's mission, then there are huge implications for God's people. Mission is not a department of the church, alongside children's work, discipleship, and worship services. It is not one of many things that the church does. It is *the* thing! Discipleship is important – it is part of growing people to be better equipped for mission. Children's work is important – they are growing as participants in God's mission. In worship we witness to who God is and what he wants for his world.

God's mission is for *all of God's people* – every member of every church.
God's mission is for *all areas of life* and for all parts of creation.
God's mission is for *all nations and peoples*.

Mission Is for Everyone

Every single one of God's people – every church member who has become part of the family of God through faith in Jesus – is called to be involved in the family business, the mission of God. Jesus commanded all of us to be salt and

---

2. Christopher J. H. Wright, *The Mission of God: Unlocking the Bible's Grand Narrative* (Downers Grove, IL: IVP Academic, 2006), 62.

light,[3] to go into all the world with the gospel.[4] He doesn't just call the church leadership or the mission committee but the whole church!

The New Testament gives us a range of different images to help us envision the life of the church. Some churches today act as if the image we are given is of a bus, with one driver and many passive passengers. Of course, the passengers pay their way, but the driver does all the work!

Some churches may have a more active view that they are cheering on a team. The key church members – people who are thought to have the real talent and aptitude for service – are in a race. But the crowd who cheer them on are seen as too ordinary and unskilled to take part in the race themselves. We do find the picture of a race in the New Testament – but we are *all* in the race, all meant to be training as athletes so we can perform well. And it is the saints in heaven who are cheering us on.[5]

We are also given the image of a body.[6] Everyone has a role to play, and everyone is interdependent. So there is diversity, but there is coordination and a unity of purpose. The role of church leadership is to equip and support church members as they live for Christ.

Mission Is Everywhere

God's mission is for all areas of life and for all parts of creation. For most of us, being part of God's mission does not mean we drop what we are doing and become involved in full-time church ministry. Mission happens where we are: in offices, schools, hospitals, homes and shops, on the streets, in the fields, at the market . . . in many areas of life, and in many parts of creation.

Many church leaders find that much of their time is spent on pastoral ministry to church members. The church members, by contrast, are out in the world, rubbing shoulders with the very people who need to experience God's love and mercy. Surely that is the most effective way of God's mission spreading to all creation. Michael Huggins, TEE pioneer in Russia, puts it this

---

3. Matthew 5:13–16.
4. Matthew 28:19–20; Mark 16:15; Luke 24:45–47; Acts 1:8.
5. Hebrews 12:1. See also 1 Corinthians 9:24; 2 Timothy 4:7.
6. Romans 12:4–8; 1 Corinthians 12:12–31; Ephesians 1:22–23; 4:15–16.

way: "Today's social-economic problems in Russia demonstrate that changing political systems does not change men's hearts. There is urgent work for the churches and every member is needed . . . God's tentmakers, God's ants, God's partisans, God's laborers rather than God's loiterers, all envisioned and equipped to change society for Jesus."[7]

Mission Is Global

God's mission has always been to reach everyone. In the Old Testament, we see that the chosen people were only chosen *for mission*, not to be part of a private club of the redeemed. It's the vision of the Old Testament from Genesis, where God promises Abraham that all nations will be blessed through him,[8] through the Psalms, where all peoples are called to praise God,[9] and into the prophets, where we see Israel called to be a light for the nations.[10]

We see this global mission in Jesus's command to make disciples of all nations and then again when he promises his Holy Spirit to help, *"and you will be my witnesses in Jerusalem, and in all Judea and Samaria, and to the ends of the earth"* (Acts 1:8 NIV). The New Testament goes on to show the beginning of this great globalization of God's mission. It ends in Revelation with a glorious picture of what will finally be – a time when an uncountable crowd "from every nation, tribe, people and language" will stand before the throne of God, giving him praise![11]

If God's mission is global, then all people everywhere must be equipped for mission. National churches will reach their own people most effectively – they need no visas, no permits, no language study, no cultural orientation. But they do need *tools* to *equip* and *empower*! And that is what TEE is all about.

---

7. Michael Huggins, "The Open Russian Theological Academy," in *Diversified Theological Education: Equipping All God's People,* ed. Ross Kinsler (Pasadena: William Carey International University, 2008), 282–83.

8. Genesis 12:3; 18:17–18.

9. E.g. Psalm 67:3; 117:1.

10. Isaiah 42:6; 49:6; 60:3.

11. Revelation 7:9.

Being part of God's mission by sharing the gospel with a friend

2

Intentional Discipleship

Penelope Vinden and Graham Aylett

Imagine that you're walking with a friend down the street. Your friend points out a certain house and says, "There is a family there with fourteen children, and the mother is now expecting another child. How do you feel about that?"

You're not too sure how to answer that question. So you ask, "How is she doing with the fourteen she already has?"

The response? "Six are doing fine, and four are more or less OK. She doesn't know where the other four are – they are missing."[1] I'd be shocked by such a situation! How could a mother not look after her children? Why would she desire more children if she is not properly nurturing and caring for the ones she already has?

Is this a picture of some of the Christian church? We want to grow in numbers, but often we are not adequately caring for the church members that God has already given us. Jesus told his followers to go and make disciples. This means more than just increasing our numbers!

What Is a Disciple?

A disciple is a *learner*. She or he is not simply learning a body of knowledge but is learning to live in a different way. Disciples of Jesus want not just Bible

---

1. From Billie Hanks Jr., heard at an Operation Multiplication training, Jakarta, Indonesia, August 2013.

knowledge or Bible skills. They are focused on becoming like Jesus – in character, thoughts, passions, motivations, and behavior.

The Urdu language has two words for a learner. One is used for a school student who learns knowledge from books in a classroom. The other is for an apprentice who learns skills and habits on the job, working with an older mentor. This second word is what the Urdu Bible translators rightly used to translate "disciple." Jesus's disciples learned as apprentices, not in the classroom.

Here is how Billy Graham described a disciple:

> A disciple is simply someone who believes in Jesus and seeks to follow him in his or her daily life. . . . It means first of all that we want to learn from him – and we will, as we study God's word. . . . But being a disciple also means we want to put God's word into action by seeking to live the way Christ wants us to live – with God's help.[2]

So a disciple is someone who not merely holds a certain set of beliefs but also lives a changed life. The Great Commission includes this aspect of whole life transformation. Jesus asks us not just to make disciples but to teach them to *do* everything he has commanded us.[3]

Church life should give new Christians models for what it means to follow Jesus. The church should be the place where discipling takes place, as those who are young in the faith look to those who have walked the path of obedience over many years. A pastor in Mongolia commented,

> If we want to assess a factory that makes shoes, we look at the shoes. How well are they made? How long do they last? And so on. How will we assess the health of a church? Should we not look at the disciples being made? How well are they made? How long do they last? And so on.[4]

---

2. Billy Graham, "What Does It Mean to Be a Disciple of Jesus?" *The Kansas City Star*, 15 May 2016.

3. Matthew 28:19–20.

4. Chinzorig pastor in an address to the Fourth Mongolian Pastors Ikh Khuraldai, Summer 2006.

How Do Disciples Grow?

Growing as Jesus's disciple means becoming more like him day by day, year by year. The Holy Spirit does this work in us, applying God's word to our lives, but we too need to join in his work by our obedience. The process is messy, uneven, and unpredictable. It has many variables, and it lasts a lifetime. What Malcolm Webber writes about an effective *leader* development process is surely also true for an effective *disciple* development process:

> An effective leader development process is not a neat series of courses but a fiery immersion in real-life, real-time experiences, reflecting the complicated and fundamentally difficult nature of Christian leadership, bringing deep heart issues to the surface to be dealt with, and compelling the participant to look utterly to God for everything in his life and ministry.[5]

New Christians read their "discipleship curriculum" from other Christians' lives. "When I asked for Bible study, I didn't want to study the book. I was studying the person discipling me," commented one Afghan. We learn by watching and imitating, not just by reading the theory. Books on their own don't make disciples. Nor do sermons.

"It takes a village to raise a child," says the African proverb. In the same way, it takes a church to raise a disciple. God never intended for us to grow in isolation. He placed us in community, and it is in community that we grow the best. How can we learn love unless we give and receive it through others? How can we learn forbearance until we rub up against irritating people? These and so many qualities can only be learned in community.

Discipleship in the Local Church

For all these reasons, the normal place to grow disciples is in the local church. Of course, Christian community also happens whenever believers come together in Bible colleges, conferences, camps, universities, and so on. But for most people most of the time, discipleship happens in the local church.

---

5. Malcom Webber, HealthyLeaders Digest email, 30 May 2018.

It is the church's responsibility to welcome new Christians, be "family" for them, nurture them, and help them put down deep roots in Christ. The church should also give them opportunities to find their gifts, grow in their calling, and impact their non-Christian workplaces. Pastors are there not like star players in a soccer team, running everywhere with the ball and exhausting themselves in the process. Rather they should be coaches who help all the members to grow and play their part.

But how can a local church design an intentional discipleship process which helps members learn from God's word, learn from each other, learn from life experience, and put all this into practice? An intentional discipleship process should include the whole discipling environment. How can accountable learning groups be formed and facilitators equipped to lead them well? How can the courses be made interesting and relevant enough to hold the attention of busy adults with many other demands on their time?

It is not easy to create this intentional discipleship process from zero, with quality course materials as part of it. It takes much time, educational expertise, funding, and other resources, and few local churches have all that on their own. Fortunately, however, proven group-based tools already exist. One of these, TEE, has for fifty years been helping local churches worldwide to make disciples and equip leaders. Read more about this in the next chapter.

3

Equipping Disciples and Leaders through TEE

Tim Green

What Is TEE?

Traditionally, TEE stands for Theological Education by Extension, but people find this hard to understand. *Theological education* sounds academic, and *extension* sounds remote. So they assume that TEE is some kind of distance learning course for people to study on their own.

In fact, TEE is not distance learning at all! It is not for isolated learners. Nor does TEE mean any of the following: evening classes at a theological institution where material is taught by lecture; a series of seminars; or typical Bible study in a group, though they share some elements.

So, what is TEE? It is a *training approach* which equips disciples and leaders in the context of their daily lives through local learning groups. And its *learning method* combines three elements in a structured, repeated pattern: 1. Personal Study; 2. Group Meetings; and 3. Practical Application.

Tools to Equip and Empower

We like to describe TEE as Tools to Equip and Empower.[1] Expanding that phrase, we can say that TEE is

> *Tools* for local churches
> *to equip and empower* all their members
> to grow in Christ and serve him actively.

Above all, TEE's purpose is practical: to help all believers to grow as disciples and workers for Jesus. God seeks not just 1 percent of Christians to be equipped as "ministers" or "missionaries" with the other 99 percent as passive spectators. Rather, he wants all of his people to grow as whole-life disciples, making him King in every part of their lives and having an impact in society. He seeks a volunteer army of ordinary people eager to be equipped as ministers in their local churches and missionaries in their local communities.

"Helping local people to do local mission through local churches – that's how the kingdom grows," says Rev Terry Barratt of Study by Extension for All Nations (SEAN) International.[2] That is the vision of TEE. It's not just an ideal but a proven reality for thousands of churches worldwide over the last fifty years.

TEE and Local Churches

TEE works best when local churches use it as the core of their intentional discipleship and training. Church leaders in different countries express their enthusiasm for TEE. Pastor Shaxlar, Vice President of the Evangelical Alliance in Azerbaijan, said, "We have read many books but when we did these courses,

---

1. This new way of describing TEE was not created by any official world body of TEE, and no such body exists. Rather in June 2011, a group of "TEE Equippers" met together under the auspices of Increase which at that time was an informal network. We agreed that "Theological Education by Extension" did not communicate the realities of modern TEE, but we also saw that TEE as an acronym was already well known and indeed embedded in the very names of many national organizations. We therefore sought a new phrase with the same acronym. Dr Paul Bendor-Samuel in 2012 suggested "Tools to Equip and Empower." Over the next few years, this phrase proved popular and spread widely, though officially TEE still stands for "Theological Education by Extension."

2. From Terry Barratt's PowerPoint "From Chaco to China," first presented in 2010 and adapted over the years.

we understood, and we learned. I know of nothing better for the training of the Azerbaijani people."[3]

A village church leader in Nepal commented, "In villages we do not get any training, and we are ministering empty-handed. . . . I was wondering how to lead all the people because we do not have anything to lean on. . . . Then I decided to do this TEE course. I was very happy because I found what I have been praying for."[4]

Bishop Alfredo Cooper, who planted and built up churches in Chile using TEE, wrote, "We hope to produce Christians who won't always be part of the problem but who will begin to be part of God's answer to the world . . . [to create] a lay training program that involves the believers in the task of disciple-making for the rest of their lives on earth."[5]

Who Is TEE For?

TEE is for all believers, men and women from every walk of life. From new believers to emerging leaders and influencers in church and society, TEE offers a connected pathway to keep people growing:

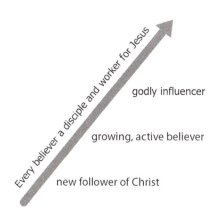

godly influencer

growing, active believer

new follower of Christ

Every believer a disciple and worker for Jesus

---

3. Pastor Shaxlar quoted in Tim Green, "Should TEE in Modern Asia be Rejected, Renewed or Merely Repackaged?" unpublished paper (2011), 31.

4. Quoted in Green, "Should TEE in Modern Asia Be Rejected," 32.

5. Alfredo Cooper, "Tools for Growth" (no date), 4, unpublished paper.

This pathway does not start with "disciples" who later become "workers for Jesus." Rather, these identities flow together. Even the newest disciple works for Jesus, while the most experienced worker must still keep growing as a disciple. When some Uighur people in Central Asia started TEE in the 1990s, they were still new in the faith. But they had a big vision: "every believer a disciple and a worker for Jesus."[6]

As people move up the pathway, they may have different circles of influence and responsibility. A new follower of Christ might especially influence their non-Christian friends; a maturing Christian might lead a cell group or Sunday school class; and a senior pastor or city mayor has a large sphere of influence.

Each believer does not grow in isolation. TEE is about committed groups of learners progressing together:

How Does TEE Work?

What makes TEE unique is its structured combination of three elements: personal study, group meetings, and practical application. These three steps link together in each learning cycle.

---

6. As described by Michael Huggins who worked with others to help pioneer TEE in Central Asia in the 1990s. He gives the full version as "every disciple a believer, and every believer a worker for Jesus." Michael Huggins, "The Open Russian Theological Academy," in *Diversified Theological Education: Equipping All God's People,* ed. Ross Kinsler, 282–83 (Pasadena: William Carey International University, 2008).

The first step is *personal study*. Participants work through a carefully prepared lesson that involves active learning, not passive reading. The lesson helps them engage with Scripture, gain new knowledge, and start to connect it with their own life experience. All this becomes a springboard to the next learning step.

Second are the *group meetings*. Here members share what they learned in the first step, reflecting on their own experience and learning from each other. They also study Scripture together. The group leader's role is to facilitate this discussion, not to give a lecture. Then members prepare for the third step by deciding how they will put the lesson into practice.

The third step is *practical application*. Whatever was learned in steps one and two must now be applied in members' daily life at home, work, church, and the wider community. Practical application is the goal of TEE courses. So this step involves a specific assignment whether for personal life or for ministry.

None of these three strands is exceptional on its own, but the TEE method weaves them together into a stronger cord. They combine into a learning cycle like this diagram illustrates.

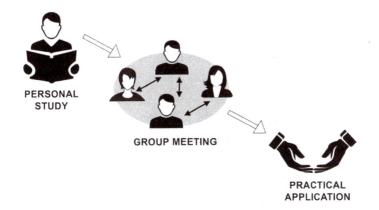

PERSONAL
STUDY

GROUP MEETING

PRACTICAL
APPLICATION

Repeated week by week, this learning cycle becomes a habit integrated into the learners' routines. Typically they complete a course in three months and then proceed to the next course. The personal study and practical application become ongoing tracks in their life, like the rails in this diagram, supported by the regular group meetings.

Busy adults can fit TEE into the fabric of their normal lives, alongside their commitments to work and family. They spend one to three hours a week in personal study and one evening at the group meeting, thus building a sustainable habit of learning.

In a structured TEE program, certificates are given to learners who attend regularly, take part in group discussions, and complete their home study and tests, although assessment for practical application is sometimes weaker. Records are kept, and the learners may reach completion points such as a certificate, diploma, or degree; in some programs, these are accredited by official accrediting bodies.

However, academic credit is not the prime purpose of TEE. Above all it is a tool for local churches to use to equip their own people. Some foundational courses can also be used in a one-to-one discipling relationship. Some learning groups draw people from different churches. Or sometimes a whole TEE course can be covered in one week at an intensive study program. So TEE has room for variety, as long as it retains and repeats the core combination of three learning steps.

Marks of Good TEE Training

TEE learners are not a captive audience. They are free adults with many claims on their time. So they will only continue in the program if they find it accessible, applicable, and affordable. It has to hold their interest by connecting truth with life, by building on their past experience, and by allowing them to contribute in a supportive group environment.

Creating this environment is the task of the group leader. He or she has to combine the *skill* of leading lively discussion with the *character* of being a good role model and the *commitment* of giving their time voluntarily every week to serve the group. Indeed, the whole TEE program stands or falls with the quality of these leaders. A well led group can thrive even if the course materials are imperfect. A badly led group will shrivel and die, even if the materials are excellent. The beating heart of TEE is not the study book but the group meeting.

Therefore, TEE organizations and churches must work hard to find, train, encourage, and support the local group leaders. Every course needs a carefully designed Leaders' Guide as well as the student book. Every single week across Asia and the Middle East, thousands of Christians give their time free of charge to lead their TEE groups. They are the indispensable frontline workers in TEE!

Disciples Who Make Disciples Who Make Disciples . . .

Churches are growing rapidly in many countries today. We need training models which can multiply disciples and workers. One approach is to establish a residential Bible school. But this requires buildings, professors, and scholarships. It takes much time and money to build a seminary or to train a professor, so it is difficult to multiply them.

Such institutions are still important, especially for equipping scholars and some leaders. But they can never meet the need of discipling all believers or equipping them for local ministries. Church-based training is better suited for this and can multiply more rapidly.

Local TEE groups require neither buildings nor professors nor scholarships. The group leaders are facilitators, not teachers. Nor do they have to create their own course content because other experts have already done it. This makes it easier to find new group leaders, though they should still be mature believers who are familiar with the course content and method.

Therefore, TEE groups can reproduce fairly rapidly. By taking part in a few courses, a TEE learner will grasp the method well. A short additional training equips that person to start a new group, which in time will spawn more groups. This book gives inspiring examples of how this multiplication has worked in practice. Whether in new, growing churches like those in Nepal and China, or in challenging contexts like Central Asia and Pakistan, TEE has again and again proved able to reproduce, multiply, and spread.

This spread does not happen automatically. Local TEE groups may falter or stagnate when badly led. Members may drop out because of life's other pressures or losing interest or moving to another town. Whole TEE programs may shrink due to financial crises, poor leadership, or conflicts on the board. There is no guarantee that a program will continue growing in healthy ways. Health and growth depend on God's Spirit and the commitment of the TEE leaders.

Nevertheless, TEE in Asia today is by and large a success story. Section B of this book tells the stories. TEE helps churches to make disciples who make disciples who make disciples!

WHAT EXCITES US ABOUT TEE

At Increase's 2010 conference in Nepal, the seventy participants were asked, "What excites you about TEE?" Their collated responses led to the following from the Kathmandu 2010 Conference Statement:

We are excited about TEE!

We have seen repeatedly, consistently and in many regions the life-changing, transforming work of God in people's lives as they study through TEE. We know the joy of seeing them grow.

We believe that TEE has a solid educational foundation combining home study, regular group meetings and practical application. The TEE method promotes immediate and ongoing application, and should lead to holistic, all-round growth, not just growth in knowledge. It is people-oriented and learner-centered. This method develops a whole range of skills: personal study skills, listening and communication skills, and skills of critical thinking and evaluation according to biblical values and a biblical worldview.

The TEE courses we use are faithful to the Scriptures, and encourage students to engage in close, deep, regular and ongoing study of God's word. They bring sound teaching, and help people to understand and apply the Bible in their context.

TEE materials can be widely used across denominations, promoting the unity of faith, and have been tried and tested in many contexts and countries. There are materials at all levels, including those that are easy to use and understand, practical and not too academic. TEE is therefore a tool for training from the ground level to the highest levels of learning. TEE learning materials can also be delivered in a great variety of ways, by printed media and multi-media electronic tools.

The TEE method allows great flexibility: groups can study anywhere at any time. It can be used in all kinds of situations, city and countryside, including in a blended form alongside residential training. It is especially appropriate where there is persecution. It is a great tool for serving diaspora communities. Because the costs to the student are low, the program is affordable. Because group meetings usually take place weekly, students can learn alongside the continuing responsibilities of their daily lives in their homes, workplaces and communities. Through a TEE program, training and learning are made accessible for everyone who wants to learn, regardless of location, salary, age or gender.

The TEE method provides training in the context of everyday life and ministry – training people where they live and work and serve – in this way integrating learning and living. TEE in Asia is indigenous, rooted in national movements, giving many opportunities for creating contextual training in partnership with the local churches.

Therefore we affirm that TEE can provide a sound framework for discipleship: spiritual formation, mentoring and character development. It can help Christians grow in the knowledge of God. It is a means to go forward in obedience to the Great Commission, as it combines materials for discipleship, training of church leaders, and church-planting. As group facilitators give rise to new facilitators there is inbuilt multiplication. It is local church related, and often local church based. Through TEE groups, relationships are deepened, and real community grows.

Above all, we believe TEE has the potential to equip all Church members as agents of transformation, moving them from being passive receivers to active servants, salt and light where they are.

That's why we are excited about TEE!

"Kathmandu 2010 Conference Statement," Increase Association, 2010, https:// increaseassociation.org/news-archive/31-kathmandu-2010-conference-statement.

4

Intelligent TEE Course Design

Tim Green

Some people evaluate a TEE course just by looking at the study book. But TEE course design involves much more than the book. It is about the whole learning experience, as we saw in chapter 3. If done well, this learning experience should be the following:

- *Rooted* in the Bible
- *Relational* with other believers in a group
- *Rounded* with integrated growth in knowledge, character, and abilities
- *Relevant* to members' context, culture, and learning style
- *Responsive* using active learning, not one-way information
- *Regular* with scheduled meetings and practical assignments
- *Reproducible* so that the learners go on to equip others in turn.

An Integrated Learning Experience

The study book plays an important part, but it is the group meeting that really grips people's hearts and strengthens their commitment. If the group is boring, members drop out. The group leader plays a really vital role. So too does the practical application, when learners immediately act on what they learned the previous week.

The best way to evaluate a TEE course is not just to look at the study book, but to attend a group meeting and ask members what change they see in their lives.

Transformation is the aim, not just information. One way to plan a course is to ask, "What *topics* should we teach?" But a better approach is to ask, "How will the *learners* be changed, and how can they bring change in their *contexts*?" Intelligent TEE design takes the second approach, from which arise four further questions:

- Who are the learners?
- What are their contexts?
- What are the course objectives?
- How will the course fulfill its objectives?

First Question: Who Are the Learners?

TEE learners give their own time and money to take part. In the midst of life's pressing demands, they struggle to find time each week to complete the personal study, the group meeting, and the practical assignment. Therefore, the learning must be enjoyable and relevant to their lives. It must also be at an appropriate academic level, with a manageable amount of work each week. It must build on their prior experience, helping them to connect life with truth, and truth with life. If these factors are not included, the learners will drop out.

Also TEE learners are extremely diverse. Wealthy and poor, urban and rural, women and men, they come from all walks of life. Some are barely literate; others have PhDs. Some are old; some young (though TEE is designed for adults, not children). Some have grown up as Christians, while others are the first in their family to convert from another religion. Some are new followers of Jesus needing discipleship, while others are already leaders in church and society. To create courses for such a huge range of learners, we can never say "one size fits all." Instead we must analyse the learners according to the different variables. For instance, we may ask where they fit on the following chart.

This diagram shows that "education level" is not necessarily related to "ministry level." Suppose a doctor (learner A) turns to Christ in midlife from a completely non-Christian background. Though highly educated, she needs to be grounded in Christian basics. Conversely, learner B shows a mature leader with much responsibility but little background education; that person will need relevant leadership training but at a relevant academic level. Around

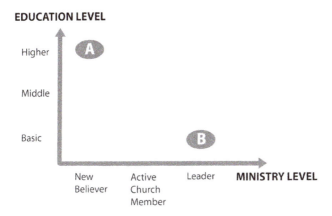

three million churches worldwide are led by pastors who have no theological training, and many of them have had no higher education. How may their needs be met through TEE?

Second Question: What Are the Learners' Contexts?

Context should always come before content in developing a TEE course. What are the learners' situations? What challenges do they and their churches face? What are the dominant religions in their country? Are the churches old or young, growing or stagnating? How can TEE learners make a difference in these contexts? What would transformation look like in church or society?

The twenty-first century is seeing a rapidly changing world: a world of conflicts, inequality, environmental challenges, continuing disease and poverty, and populations on the move. All Christ's followers are called to play their part in God's mission for transformation, in society as well as in the church. Most TEE learners are ordinary working people embedded in the fabric of their situations. So TEE should equip them to make a difference. But what kind of difference? This leads us to the next question.

Third Question: What Are the Course Objectives?

Educationalists typically describe three areas or "domains" of learning. The *cognitive* domain concerns head knowledge and mental processes. The *affective* domain is about emotions, values, and attitudes. The *psychomotor* domain is about physical skills but often includes broader abilities and may be called the behavioral domain. In simpler language, we can label these three domains as *knowing, being,* and *doing.* Therefore, our course objectives focus on what the learner should *know, be,* and be able to *do* by the end of the course.

These three widely recognized categories have stood the test of time. However, they were created in individualistic Western societies and just focus on the individual. Most TEE learners, by contrast, are members of collectivist societies where the group is extremely important. TEE learning fits well with this context because it is group based. So in addition to the important domains of knowing, being, and doing, we add a fourth: relating. How do our TEE courses equip learners to relate to other people in the church community and in their wider circles of family, workplace, and nation?

Part C of this book explains how the Increase Association equips new course writers in Asia to analyze their twenty-first century contexts and their learners' needs in those contexts to develop course objectives. It is exciting to see new transformative material being written.

Fourth Question: How Will the Course Fulfill Its Objectives?

In a classroom setting, a teacher is face to face with the learners and can read their body language. Are they looking bored? Then the well-trained teacher will inject a learning activity. Do the students have a puzzled expression on their faces? The alert teacher will find out why. Also a good teacher will use not just lectures, but interactive exercises as part of dynamic learning. This learning will be followed after the class by self-study to reinforce the lesson.

TEE similarly uses a mix of methods for dynamic learning, but in a different order. The self-study phase comes before the class interaction, not after it. This "flipped classroom" approach has been promoted as a new educational breakthrough, although TEE discovered it fifty years ago! It enables learners to grasp the key teaching points beforehand, thus freeing up the group time for discussion, not lecture. This approach is especially relevant for adult learners who have a rich store of life experience to share in the discussions.

TEE course design, when done well, fulfills the different objectives in an integrated way. The *knowing* objectives are mostly fulfilled in the personal study step. Many (not all) TEE study books teach new knowledge in short steps whereby learners grasp the key teaching points through reading, responding, and review. Concrete examples help him or her to connect these points to real life. Further reinforcement happens when the learner completes a simple test and can explain the points to others.

Often this stepwise learning method is called "programmed learning," but it is the material that is programmed, not the student! To be sure, there is a risk of the latter when programmed learning is done too rigidly. But if combined with critical reflection, it still plays a valuable role because it helps learners grasp key points with confidence. However, programmed instruction is not an essential part of TEE. Some courses use it and others do not, especially at higher academic levels where longer written assignments are needed.

In a good course, the TEE study book also begins to address the *being* objectives. Some questions are included for personal reflection. For example, "Have you ever faced a situation like that?" or "Stop now and talk with God about it." Such questions help the teaching to seep through from head to heart. This process unfolds even more in the group discussion time which stirs emotions, memories, and willpower.

The discussion time is also important for *relating* as members learn to play their part in the group: contributing their opinion appropriately, listening to others, caring, and praying for each other. Relating also happens beyond the group as learners interact with families and neighbors. Some practical assignments especially focus on this relating. For example in a TEE lesson on husbands and wives, the assignment is "Do something to make your spouse happy this week, and be ready to talk about it in next week's group meeting."

Doing objectives are also normally met through the practical application step. The assignment may be for a learners' personal growth, or their relationship with others, or a ministry skill related to the course topic. For example, TEE courses on preaching include an assignment where each learner takes a turn preaching a sermon and receiving feedback on it. In Pakistan, a course for young people on caring for their environment includes a group assignment where learners pick up litter on the street and afterwards discuss their feelings.

Fifty years of TEE have seen some excellent courses developed and some very poor ones. In the next chapter, we see how the best courses have spread and borne fruit, while the worst have died.

5

The Worldwide Spread of TEE

Tim Green and David Ball

This chapter briefly describes how the TEE movement has evolved over the last half century. The first wave began as hands-on training for pastors in local churches. The second wave, starting two decades later, spread as a tool to also equip ordinary church members. A third wave is just beginning now.

A First Wave of TEE from the 1960s

TEE was born in 1964 as an experiment to overcome failure. A seminary in the Central American country of Guatemala had discovered that very few of their graduates returned to the rural pastoral ministries for which they had been trained. Meanwhile the local leaders of rural congregations received no training. What should be done? An "extension" branch of the seminary started, with the teachers travelling out regularly to equip the rural pastors in their own contexts. And so "Theological Education by Extension" (TEE) was born.

The concept of TEE spread rapidly to other continents in the early 1970s. At first it was an extension of a seminary with the same purpose of preparing pastors, but using different methodologies in different locations. A creative burst of TEE course writing led to many new courses in different languages. It was a time of heady excitement, when some predicted that TEE would displace residential training.

However, to launch a TEE program is one thing; to sustain it is another. Sustaining requires good leadership, ownership by churches, adequate finances, interesting course materials, and excellent local facilitators. When these requirements were not met, many TEE programs faltered and some died. Many of the early TEE course materials failed the standard. Some study books were too difficult or theoretical. Some had poor questions or unattractive formatting. Some were just boring. Some courses were issued without a leader's guide and thus failed to help the local group leaders on whom so much depends. Over time many courses fell into disuse.

However, some programs flourished. "Survival of the fittest" meant that the more interesting, understandable, and applicable courses spread widely because TEE students enjoyed them. In some parts of Asia, courses from the first wave of TEE that were written in their contexts are still enjoyed today and have been revised along the way. In Africa, a successful curriculum of forty TEE courses is called TEXT Africa. The courses were specifically written for African contexts and have proven their ongoing value. In Latin America, the curriculum written by SEAN became so globally influential that it needs to be described in more detail.

Study by Extension for All Nations (SEAN)

The TEE courses Abundant Life, Abundant Light and the integrated two-year ministry training course called The Life of Christ, as well as many other courses, are produced by an organization called SEAN (pronounced "Say-ann"). The story of SEAN begins in South America where Anglicans were working with indigenous people in Chile, Paraguay, and the northern plains of Argentina.

In the 1960s, they were blessed by growth with new believers and new churches each year. But who would lead the new churches? There were no ordained indigenous pastors and no established training program. How could they make the transition from missionary leadership to national leadership? In the cities, more established denominations had their Bible schools and seminaries. But none of the leaders from the new tribal churches could even dream of going to a seminary. The expense, the academic level, and the practicality of leaving home and livelihood all made it impossible.

And so was born **Se**minario por **E**xtensión **AN**glicano, or SEAN. The word "sean" means "to be" in Spanish, as in 2 Timothy 2:2, to "be qualified to teach others."

SEAN was formally established on 14 July 1971. The first step was to make a very careful analysis of the field needs. The second step was to create study texts written specially for the local situations by gathering a team of teachers to develop programed self-study materials combined

SEAN's Origins

with weekly group tutorials. The third step was to take the course materials out to the churches.

Gradually, under the leadership of Rev Tony Barratt, the new SEAN team developed tailor-made materials – initially Abundant Life for new believers and The Life of Christ for potential Christian workers and leaders. These courses were tested in depth with different groups in the cities and in rural areas. The system worked: leaders were trained and began to take on the pastoring of churches. Tony and his team continued to write new special programed courses and leaders' manuals as they were needed. And so the program grew.

The project was based on three fundamental principles. The courses had to be the following:

1. *Simple* – Traditional theological education was aimed at those with formal education, on the higher levels of the educational ladder. SEAN

**SEAN materials
in the early days**

was aimed at those who had little or no formal education and spoke Spanish as their second language.

2. *Biblical* – Every effort was made to give clear biblical exegesis, providing different interpretations and leaving controversial points open-ended for each denomination to explain their own position.

3. *Practical* – SEAN's training expected people to apply their learning in their own discipleship and in the ministry of the church. It is only when we pass on what we learn that it becomes effective.

SEAN never publicized its courses, but gradually word spread from mouth to mouth, thus creating an ever increasing demand from potential users, first in Argentina and Chile and then all over the world. Printing, storage, and dispatching material became a hugely challenging task for the small team. Eventually, SEAN decided to concentrate only on writing courses and to license other people as partners to print and use them.

SEAN also received requests for the courses to be translated into different languages. Licenses were given for groups to translate the courses, make appropriate illustrations, and give examples for the local context. The blessing flowed in the other direction too, as courses written in Asia were published by SEAN for worldwide use. Because of expansion to other countries and denominations, SEAN changed its name to Study by Extension for All Nations.

As SEAN's courses became more widely known, the Christian and Missionary Alliance (C&MA) encouraged the use of SEAN courses among their churches in many Asian countries including Laos, Cambodia, the Philippines,

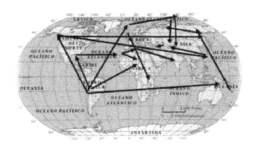

SEAN map showing how the courses spread

Thailand, and Vietnam. By 1976, SEAN's The Life of Christ course was adapted for India and is now available in twelve Indian languages. SEAN's courses were also adapted for Pakistan, Bangladesh, Nepal, Russia, Central Asia, and indeed most of the countries in part B of this book.

At present SEAN materials are used in more than one hundred countries and have been translated into over eighty languages. Some people have even gained the impression that SEAN is the same as TEE. Actually, SEAN is only one of many course providers, albeit the most influential one.

A Second Wave of TEE from the 1980s

With some exceptions, the first wave of TEE aimed to equip pastors, but by the 1980s, a second wave was beginning that eventually outgrew the first. SEAN's growth contributed much to this by making TEE courses easier for ordinary people to enjoy, and some of TEXT Africa's courses also spread. This second wave sought to equip all kinds of Christians, not just leaders.

This chart need not imply that today's TEE courses are "beneath" the level of educated church members. It simply means they are more accessible to all. Many times, educated Christians in Asia express surprise at how much they

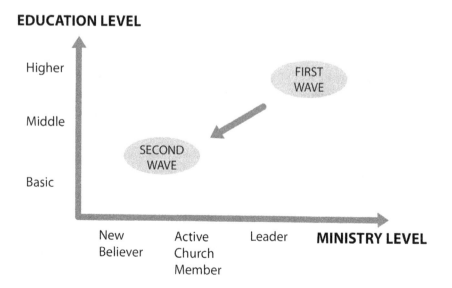

learn from apparently simple courses once they engage with them fully. The courses also give them a framework to explain biblical truth to others.

In the 1990s, the second wave accelerated further to wherever multitudes were turning to Christ from other religions. In countries like China, Mongolia, and Nepal, new churches were springing up like mushrooms after rain. How could the new believers be discipled well? How could local leaders be equipped for the new churches? And how could all this be done in an affordable way in local contexts? In response to these issues, dozens of new national TEE movements were formed to meet the urgent needs on the ground. This second wave of TEE continues to this day.

Creative Synergy with Theological Institutions

Sometimes TEE and residential seminaries have been viewed as rivals. Actually, they can work in creative partnership riding on the second wave of TEE which has made the courses so useful for equipping all believers. This means that pastors now have a ready tool to equip and empower all their members more deeply than through sermons alone. Preaching is of course vitally important, but listeners to God's word also need to become doers of the word. Seminaries can enhance the future impact of their students by training them to use TEE and similar tools for active Christian growth, just as they rightly train them to preach good sermons. In places where this is already happening, seminary leaders are delighted by the outcome.

The second wave of TEE can also help theological institutions by giving them a ready flow of students in places where enrolment is falling. When hundreds of church members gain an appetite for biblical studies through TEE, some will be called to continue on to higher study. This increases not only the quantity of students that seminaries intake, but also their quality, since these are mature Christians who have already proved their commitment to study and to God's church.

Finally, the blended learning design of TEE can greatly help seminaries that are developing extension programs for the Christian public. Since contact time with such students is so limited and precious, the impact can be increased by moving informational content away from class time and thus freeing it up for interactive learning. The TEE movement can help such programs through experience in educational design. Meanwhile, the TEE movement also stands to benefit from seminaries in ways explored in part C of this book.

An Emerging Third Wave of TEE in the Twenty-First Century

If the first wave of TEE sought to equip leaders for pastoral ministry, as it still does today in many places, and the second wave expanded this equipping to all believers, then may we discern an emerging third wave? Each wave does not displace the one before it but rolls out further into new areas. Today, at least in Asia, a third wave is gathering momentum and opening up new horizons.

This third wave is marked by innovation as national Christians lead TEE movements and take it in new directions. Creative new courses are being written for local contexts. New connections are being made between TEE organizations, leading to new collaborative initiatives. There is potential for partnerships with seminaries and joined-up learning pathways. In some places, TEE for teenagers is being developed, as well as TEE for oral preference learners and digital courses. TEE is also reaching the diaspora in growing numbers. New energy is in the air.

These new horizons are too wide for individual TEE organizations to explore on their own. This is where the work of the Increase Association is crucial because it links church-based training programs throughout Asia and the Middle East. As they collaborate, these national programs can achieve so much more. All the national TEE programs in part B of this book are members of the Increase Association. Part C describes some ways in which Increase is fostering innovation in twenty-first century TEE.

WHAT IS THE INCREASE ASSOCIATION?

Increase is an association of church-based training organizations rooted in and around Asia, most of whom use TEE. Increase is governed by an Asian committee and has a small serving base in Malaysia. It is an associate member of the Asia Theological Association (ATA).

Increase's vision is to see churches equipping all Christ's followers in their contexts, so that many millions are discipled and empowered for mission, ministry, and leadership.

Increase's purpose is to connect and strengthen church-based training movements across Asia and beyond. Together they do the following:

- Build a network of good relationships.
- Encourage collaborative projects and partnerships.
- Initiate and catalyze innovative approaches.
- Identify and share fruitful practice.
- Provide support, resources, advice, and training.
- Make a global contribution to theological education and adult learning.
- Connect with other church-based training associations and accrediting associations.
- Communicate widely the news and stories from Increase members.

Increase's work is carried out mostly by its members on a voluntary basis. For instance the Increase Equippers are experienced practitioners willing to pass on their experience through training workshops and consultancy visits. Task groups focus on particular areas of innovation. The intercessors team support the work in prayer and the Increase Trust UK in finance. The small serving base is in Malaysia, and the Increase committee gives oversight to the whole work.

The values of Increase guide their work:
- Sharing – through relationships and networking
- Inclusive – of all people, cultures, and denominations
- Servant-hearted – in leadership and with each other
- Learning and changing – together and from each other
- Relevant – to local cultures and contexts
- Biblical – in how we work and act.

Read more in http://www.increaseassociation.org.

Part B

TEE in and around Asia

ASIA

6

TEE in Asia Today

Tim Green

This chapter introduces part B of this book where we tell the stories of twenty-one countries and people groups in which TEE organizations are helping churches to make disciples and grow their own leaders. All of these movements are members of the Increase Association in and around Asia. Part C will explain how these diverse TEE organizations are connected through Increase, which not only helps them to strengthen each other but also to explore new horizons of innovation in twenty-first century TEE.

Why Asia Matters

Today, no one can ignore Asia. More people live there than in all other continents combined. East Asia is an economic powerhouse, and China is a new superpower. Some of the world's wealthiest people live in Asia as do some of the poorest, and the gap is growing. Yet even the poor have smartphones. They can roam the world and glimpse new horizons with their fingers. Meanwhile, nationalistic governments are using increasingly sophisticated surveillance to monitor their citizens and to clamp down on dissent.

Asia is the heartland of world religions. Hinduism, Buddhism, and Islam were all formed here. Nearly all Asians receive a religious label at birth and imbibe its values with their mother's milk. In some regions, atheistic communism replaced the old religions with a new ideology, but it is now looking a little threadbare. Meanwhile in all parts of Asia, the internet allows young people to explore religious options more easily than before, whether openly or in secret.

Where does Christianity fit? Statistically, Asia is the least Christianized continent. In some places, ancient Christian communities have survived for centuries, though now are drastically reduced in the Middle East. In other countries, missionary established churches have gained a foothold. In general, however, Christianity has been viewed as a Western religion, a foreign import which "does not belong here."

But that's only half the story! Or even less than half, because there are huge, vigorous movements of people coming to Christ in country after country. Fifty years ago, the church in China was almost crushed out of existence. Today Christians number at least one hundred million! Missionaries from mainland China may be at the forefront of global outreach in the coming decades. In Hindu Nepal, Buddhist Mongolia, and Muslim Iran, we hear similar stories of astonishing growth. Across Asia, the growing edge of God's kingdom is occupied by first-generation Christians.

Intrepid Gospel Pioneers

In Asia today there are still roles for expatriate missionaries, but the dynamic growth is led by national believers themselves. Let's hear about three of them who are unsung heroes of the gospel.

In remote rural Nepal, God called a former Hindu named Ram to plant churches. But how could Ram be trained? Seminary in the city was too far away, too expensive, and too academic. Besides, as a former leprosy patient, Ram had lost all of his fingers. But help was at hand right in his home church! The regular TEE training gave Ram confidence to start planting churches. Within eight years, he had planted seventeen churches in the remote hills, one of which grew to five hundred members. He is now equipping the next generation of leaders using the same TEE method which trained him so effectively.[1]

---

1. Tanka Subedi, Director of ITEEN, Institute for Theological Education by Extension in Nepal, at the "Discipling the Nations" event, Kuala Lumpur, 22 April 2015, and on subsequent occasions.

In Central Asia, Adil and Nurjan[2] (not their real names) both grew up as Muslims, and Adil became an imam in a mosque. But Jesus changed their lives, and now they reach out to their own people. They planted one fellowship of former Muslims and use TEE to strengthen the believers. Now they are preparing someone else to take on the leadership so they can move on to a new place and plant a new church. Nurjan said, "We don't want to stay in comfortable places. In our past our people were nomads, and we are children of Abraham. We move on to reach new people. We trust God."[3]

In Mongolia, Okhio grew up as a Buddhist and was one of the first in his country to respond to the gospel in 1990. From then till now, he has planted no less than fifty-five churches! One of the smallest consists of a few herdsmen living on the edge of the Gobi Desert, three full days' drive from his home. Although he can only visit them twice a year, he has showed them how to feed themselves as a self-sustaining TEE group so they can continue to grow spiritually in his absence.[4]

What do these gospel pioneers have in common?

- All of them are first-generation believers in Asia's non-Christian heartlands.
- All of them are indigenous missionaries, citizens of their soil, not expatriates.
- All of them are sacrificially passionate to share Christ with their own people.
- All of them use TEE groups to make disciples and equip local leaders, which is one reason why TEE is growing in Asia today.

The Challenges of Growth

Every year in Asia, several million people become Christ's followers, and many thousands of new churches are launched. Explosive church growth is an exciting problem to have. But it brings its own challenges. One Iranian church leader said, "We can't cope with the need to nurture, train, and gather

---

2. Names have been changed for security reasons.
3. Personal communication to Tim Green, between 2012 and 2017.
4. Personal communication to Tim Green, March 2017.

the new believers. . . . Unless we find a way to cope with the fruit, we have no choice but to stop witnessing."[5] Another Iranian pastor declared, "Evangelism is useless . . . without discipleship."[6] But how can new believers be equipped as whole-life disciples with transformed lives? How may they be gathered into local groups, and who will lead these new fellowships?

One strategy is to set up residential Bible colleges which then raise money for young leaders to come for two or three years of full-time study. God has blessed this approach in many places, and such institutions are certainly needed. But there can be downsides as well in the ways candidates are selected, extracted from their contexts, and made financially dependent. In any case, how will leaders be trained on the scale that is needed? In at least three million churches worldwide, the leaders have no training!

One Asian church leader said,

> Most of the pastors and church planters working here have no formal theological training. Most of them just get a little short-term training, and then they do the ministry. As a result, when the church is growing, they face many challenges in leading the church. Besides, they are not able to train others effectively. Therefore, the church becomes lacking in workers and leaders.[7]

This diagram summarizes the need. TEE can offer part of the answer.

GROWTH

new believers | new churches

make disciples | train some as leaders

in and for the context!

---

5. In the publicity of an Iranian ministry organization, around 2008.

6. Personal communication to Tim Green at the Leader Development Consultation, Chiang Mai, May 2017.

7. Personal communication to the authors, between 2005 and 2015.

National TEE Movements in Asia

The first wave of TEE in Asia was initiated mostly by Western missionaries and served regions which already had Christian populations including Indonesia, the Philippines, the Indian subcontinent, and the Near East. Some of these early programs survived; many did not. The second wave grew later in response to the challenges of rapid church growth in new regions of Asia. This time the impetus came from national Christians and Eastern missionaries, especially Koreans. Of all the local TEE group leaders in Asia today, about 99.8 percent are Asian.[8]

The second wave has overtaken the first. Now at least one hundred thousand Asian Christians[9] are in regular TEE groups, and the growth continues. A large proportion are believers of non-Christian backgrounds who are keen to grow in their new faith and share it with others. Most of the group members and their leaders are lay people with ordinary jobs.

These everyday Christians in their everyday lives are uniquely placed to reach their neighbors of other faiths. They know their language and culture from the inside, and they need no visa. It is primarily through them that the gospel advances in Asia today. The millions who know Christ can reach the billions who don't.

TEE is a strategic tool to help Asian churches mobilize their own members at the cutting edge of Christian witness. In 2016, visitors to Pakistan asked a Christian woman what difference TEE has made to her. While they spoke, the Muslim call to prayer was ringing out from a nearby mosque. The woman replied, "Living in this context, these courses help me respond to questions and express my faith."[10] This is mission on the front lines.

In summary, TEE in Asia can strengthen Christian witness in two ways. One way is to serve new church movements at the growing edge of mission. The other is to strengthen the faith of Christians in places like Pakistan or

---

8. This is just an approximate estimate, reckoning that about twenty out of ten thousand local TEE groups in Asia are led by non-Asians. A larger number of the group leaders are Asian missionaries in other Asian countries, while the largest number are nationals of those countries.

9. Based on a survey in 2010 and subsequent estimates in 2015 and 2017. The figures are not precise, but Increase plans a more thorough analysis in 2021.

10. Personal communication to Graham Aylett during an ATA accreditation visit to the Open Theological Seminary, Lahore, in 2016.

Borneo where they inherited a "Christian" cultural identity but their own untaught faith is as fragile as an empty eggshell, liable to be crushed by pressure or inducements from a dominant religious community. But regular, biblical, obedience-oriented discipleship through TEE can give them the resilience and strength of a rubber ball.

Member Movements of the Increase Association

As this chart shows, the second wave TEE movement in Asia is still strongly growing.[11]

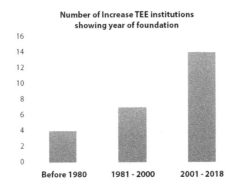

Number of Increase TEE institutions showing year of foundation

Additionally, Increase welcomes church-based training organizations which are not TEE but which fulfill the following criteria:
- Their work is nationally governed.
- Their training program is ongoing, systematic, and Bible based.
- They use active learning methods and interactive learning with others.
- Their program is rooted in the local context and the local church.
- They serve in "greater Asia" or among its peoples worldwide.

One example is Hasat, a fine indigenous organization serving local churches across Turkey. It fulfills the above criteria but does not use TEE methodology. Hopefully the Increase Association can include more such church-based

---

11. Based on information collected by Graham Aylett and last updated in 2018.

training programs in future to foster mutually beneficial interaction with the TEE movement. However, this current book is about the TEE organizations in particular.

The Stories in This Book

The stories in part B are about countries where one or more Increase member organizations are serving through TEE. They cover a surprisingly large part of Asia, as shown in dark grey on the map at the beginning of part B. The countries in lighter grey are where TEE work is starting to emerge but a national movement is not yet formalized – countries like Myanmar, Laos, and Japan. Some TEE is even happening in countries we cannot mark on the map for security reasons. Please include them in your prayers alongside the more visible movements described in these chapters.

The twenty-one story chapters are grouped in sections to illustrate different ways that TEE is being used:

- First-Generation Christians
- Discipling the Diaspora
- Christians under Pressure
- Building Stronger Churches
- Channels of Transformation

However, the categories are not watertight because most TEE programs serve more than one of these training needs. At the end of each of these chapters, we invite you to respond by praying for that TEE organization and perhaps by getting in touch with them using the contact details provided. If using the contact information does not work, write to the Increase Association, increaseassociation@gmail.com, and we will forward your enquiry.

A group of first generation Christians in Bangladesh studying a TEE course

First-Generation Christians

When people from a different religious background become Christ's followers, they can be called first-generation Christians. They may face pressure from their non-Christian families and communities as well as struggles in adapting to their new church culture. TEE groups can help provide a caring community and a context for worldview transformation. This section describes TEE movements in a sample of Buddhist and Muslim countries, but it could also have included Hindu Nepal and atheist China.

THAILAND

7

Thailand
Growing Together in Christ

Hanna-Ruth van Wingerden

Background[1]

Thailand was in the news in the summer of 2018 when a group of teenagers was stuck in a cave without food or light. Spiritually, there are many people in the dark without food or light in this country where less than 1 percent are Protestant Christians. The great majority are Buddhist. Nearly every village has at least one temple-monastery. The monks are known for their yellow robes and lead the collective rituals in temples. Even though nearly everyone is Buddhist, other religions do exist. In Bangkok and in the southern part of the country, a Muslim minority is present. Only a very small number of Thai have become Catholic or Protestant Christians, even though missionaries came to Thailand as early as the sixteenth century, and many of these Christians belong to ethnic minorities like the Sino-Thai.

Thailand is home to people of various cultures and languages. This diversity is common in many Southeast Asian countries because for centuries, people migrated throughout Asia, while political boundaries were formed later. Within the borders of Thailand, people are also on the move. Many people in the

---

1. The information in this section is from "Thailand," Wikipedia, https://en.wikipedia.org/wiki/Thailand, accessed August 2018; and "Thailand, Encyclopaedia Britannica," https://www.britannica.com/place/Thailand, accessed August 2018.

villages leave their homes to work in the cities for a few months each year. Some of these never leave the city again and view themselves as urban nowadays, though others still have strong connections to their village community.

TEE in Thailand

Churches sometimes have a pastor but suffer from a lack of people who are equipped to serve alongside them. Many churches are closed down or not able to grow due to lack of leadership. Most believers have little knowledge of the Bible: they are first-generation believers, and the Christian faith and the Bible are completely new to them. Some want to go to a seminary but are not able do so because of responsibilities for their families and jobs.

The Center for Leadership Development (CLD) is offering TEE courses throughout Thailand. CLD was established by Christian and Missionary Alliance workers in 2003 to answer the need for more lay leaders in the churches. Most churches in Thailand do not have a plan to develop lay leaders beyond evangelism and new believer discipleship. Through TEE, the new leaders will gain the necessary biblical and theological knowledge together with practical ministry skills. So far sixty churches have benefitted from CLD. Over the lifetime of the program, over five hundred people have registered, and more than eighty have graduated. CLD is one of Increase's core members, and current Director Lee Her was a member of the planning committee for Increase's latest conference in 2017.

Testimonies to TEE's Impact

Dr Jerry Yer Soung, co-founder of CLD, shares,

> At first many of the TEE graduates were not yet learning to apply the lessons to their own lives. So we brought the idea of coaching to the program: sitting one-on-one with each student, every month, and talking about the things they don't understand, meeting with them personally, talking through the important spiritual issues hidden in their hearts. They repent of their sins, and we pray for them. So TEE is the process of changing from the inside out.

Others will be transformed when they see the transformation that took place in our lives. TEE programs can only be effective when lives are being transformed.[2]

TEE students are really benefitting from the courses. As one of them explains,

I studied the Bible by correspondence in the past, and there wasn't anyone who could explain things to me. I had to figure out the meaning of passages based on my own thinking. Studying TEE courses helps me to understand the background of the Bible – the history of how things came about, the various periods of time – and see a better picture of the Bible. The method of studying alone and then discussing what you learn in small groups really adds to the implementation of new knowledge: meeting in our small groups brings us closer together. As a group we discover different areas in our lives that need to be developed or worked on. Alone, we may never realize these in ourselves, but meeting as a group we are able to help each other in these areas.[3]

Dr Jerry Yer Soung continues:

What has excited me about TEE? That I can see people's lives being changed. In the days when I was a seminary student, I did tests, I studied, there was paperwork, but my life wasn't changed until someone sat down with me and talked with me about the spiritual issues that were important for me. That was what changed me. So I am so excited about TEE, and I hope you are too. I think that if you want to use the TEE program, you need to allow God to change you first, or you'll not be able to help others change.

---

2. Dr Jerry Yer Soung in a Bible devotion at the Increase conference "Twenty-First Century TEE in Asia: Challenges and Opportunities," Kathmandu, 4–8 October 2010.

3. Quoted in "Introduction to CLD," Center for Leadership Development (CLD), http://www.sspthai.org/wordpress/about/.

In Thailand there is a mountain called Phu Chifa. On the other side is the country where I was born. My friends wanted me to see the Mekong River from the mountain top, so I agreed to climb the mountain with them. But the mountain was very high and the road very long, about ten kilometres. After one kilometre, I was so tired, and my heart was beating fast, and I couldn't go any further. But my friend resisted and said: "It is very beautiful up there. We want you to see it. We will push you, pastor! Come on!" After another couple of kilometres, I was so tired, and so four or five of them came to push me along! It was worth it when I got to the top! I could see the Mekong River, in the land where I was born! I was breathing the fresh air! It was so nice! I think TEE is like this. It is about pushing people up the mountain to a place where they can see the beautiful life that happens only when Jesus Christ transforms their lives. In the end, when they finish the program, everybody is happy. They'll have Jesus Christ in their life, and they will be ready to train others.[4]

Growing TEE

Training leaders so they can train others is one of the core strategies in TEE in Thailand. CLD wants to see every leader build another leader. The goal of being trained as a leader is to take that training, knowledge, and experience and train another leader. This curriculum is designed so that a student who has studied already can easily take what they have learned and teach someone else. While the student is in the process of studying, they should consider who they would like to train in the future. This grows and builds up the church of Thailand.

Rev Somjai Kittuk is working in a church where some people have had TEE training:

I clearly see that those who never dared to speak are now bold enough to speak and express themselves. Those who never thought they could help teach are now able to stand up and teach the

---

4. Soung, Bible devotion, Kathmandu, 2010.

Bible. Those who never thought they would stand before the congregation are now able to help me preach. Our church never had a ministry team, but now we have several teams serving side by side with me.[5]

This reverend is just one among the pastors of the churches who have seen the fruits of TEE in Thailand.

Lee Her is a missionary for the Christian and Missionary Alliance and the current Director of CLD. She has a vision for growth that could involve offering courses at two levels – not only the current leadership level, but also an additional level for all church members.

Pray and Connect

Please pray
- for further involvement of Thai church leaders in CLD;
- for revising TEE courses to make them even more effective.

Center for Leadership Development (CLD)
Website: http://www.sspthai.org/wordpress. Their website includes a video that explains the work.

---

5. Somjai Kittuk, "Stories," Center for Leadership Development, http://www.sspthai.org/wordpress/stories/.

BANGLADESH

8

Bangladesh
Life Building Courses

Graham Aylett and Hanna-Ruth van Wingerden

Background[1]

Bangladesh borders India and Myanmar. With a population of over 165 million, it is one of the most populated countries in the world. Nine out of ten people are Muslim, so Bengali Muslims are the largest people group, and Bangladesh is the third-largest country where Islam is the official religion. About 9.5 percent of the people are Hindu, and only 0.3 percent are Christian.

The Bengal Delta made by the Ganges and Brahmaputra rivers takes up most of the country. This makes Bangladesh very vulnerable to flooding, an increasing problem as sea levels rise and more rain falls due to climate change. Agriculture still makes up the largest part of the economy, and the clothing industry is the biggest industry and employs many people. Levels of education have been quite low, but are improving. More people are learning how to read and to have the opportunity to receive education.

Christians in Bangladesh come from a number of backgrounds. The forefathers of most of today's traditional Christians came to Christ from a Hindu background. Many churches still use the *William Carey Bible* that was

---

1. The facts in this section are from "Bangladesh," Wikipedia, https://en.wikipedia.org/wiki/Bangladesh;"Bangladesh," Encyclopaedia Britannica, https://www.britannica.com/place/Bangladesh/; and the College of Christian Theology Bangladesh (CCTB).

the result of the work of Baptist missionary William Carey in the nineteenth century. There are also many believers from ethnic groups like the Santal and the Garo, where a high proportion are at least nominally Christian. Still others have come to Christian faith from a Muslim background. Living in their Muslim context, all of these believers face the challenges of shaping a Christ-honoring personal, family, and community life. Those who have come to faith from a Muslim background may find the "Christian culture" and terminology of traditional Christians hard to relate to. In all groups, nominalism is one of the main problems. In nominal Christian communities, there is very little knowledge and understanding of the Bible.

TEE in Bangladesh: CCTB

There are two TEE programs serving the churches in Bangladesh, and they reach out to believers from different backgrounds. The largest and longest serving program is the College of Christian Theology Bangladesh (CCTB), which celebrated their 50th anniversary in 2018. CCTB offers a three-stage bachelors in theology (BTh) program, where the first two stages can be studied through TEE and the third stage is offered residentially just outside Dhaka, the capital city. The Acting Principal, Rev James Halder, estimates that around 60 percent of evangelical Christian leaders in Bangladesh today have benefitted from TEE training received through CCTB. One of the leaders of a Baptist denomination shared that "Local leaders and evangelists embraced TEE and are studying the courses passionately. As a result, people are coming to Christ. The Lord's kingdom is expanding through the TEE program in Bangladesh."[2]

Teaching Cleaners, Police Officers, and Bank Managers[3]

James, a church secretary, studies TEE courses from CCTB. He says,

2. John Sagar Karmakar, Increase conference "Empowering Churches, Equipping Disciples," Chiang Mai, 13–17 November 2017.

3. The content of this section is based on personal communication to Tim Green and Graham Aylett.

I have already finished four courses, and I feel more confident to carry out my church responsibilities. Before I used to preach using other people's sermons, and I never felt satisfaction and peace in my heart. Now I prepare my own sermons and preach with confidence and faith. I really notice the difference this makes. TEE group study helps me a lot to understand the Bible and interpret it in a good way. I thank God for this opportunity.

One of the staff members at CCTB is Wailes, a Christian from the Garo ethnic group. Coming from a nominal Christian background, as a young man Wailes knew of Jesus, but he had not personally encountered Jesus. That changed when one night, Wailes had a dream.

I was standing and enjoying the nice breeze in an open field, but slowly the breeze turned to a warm wind that became warmer, and then I sensed it burning on my skin, and I saw fire from the north sky, coming toward me from all sides! I tried to run, but already I was surrounded by the fire. I was trying to escape, but there was no way, and I was sure I was going to die. While I was in that agony, I heard a voice: "Jesus is coming!" And then I became more afraid, because I realized there was no Jesus in my life. I cried out to Jesus: "Please do not come now because I haven't received you yet!" I woke up crying with terrible fear. This experience led me to Jesus. I surrendered my life to Jesus.[4]

Wailes has led TEE groups with both groups of people who are poorly and more highly educated.

I had one group of students from a Harijan (low-caste Hindu) background. They worked in a hospital as sweepers. Since TEE is so flexible, I was able to organize group meetings around their working hours, even if that meant studying at night. It was exciting to see how they took the opportunity to share with their non-believing co-workers the things they had learned from the group

---

4. Personal communication to the authors.

meetings. If they faced any difficult questions, we would discuss them at the next group meeting and help them find the answers.

And speaking of another group, he says,

Ten years ago, most of my group members were college and university students. They came from different disciplines and backgrounds. As they finished their university and college degrees, we journeyed together in our TEE group. Some of them became bank managers or graphic designers, and one of them became a police inspector. Today they are really serving the community, serving society with a good reputation. I really believe that because of TEE, they became good believers and are making a positive impact on their society. That is why I know that TEE is a great tool which can be accessed by everybody.[5]

TEE in Bangladesh: SKT

First-generation Muslim background believers face particular challenges in Bangladesh. There are many obstacles and questions. How can I believe when everyone else around me does not? How can I withstand pressure to return to Islam? What can I tell my family and friends? What is God calling me to do in my life? These believers are often more comfortable with a different Christian vocabulary that is more closely related to their background, so a different TEE program was developed to serve their particular needs. This is the Shikkha Kalyan Trust (Learning for Living Educational Welfare Trust), or SKT. This seminary has courses for new believers from a Muslim background and courses to help growing believers into effective ministry. At present, SKT has ninety-eight men and women in eighteen TEE groups. As the church is growing in Bangladesh, the need for educated pastors, elders, and church workers is also rising.

---

5. Personal communication to the authors.

Understanding God's Plan for People[6]

One believer who found help from SKT courses, Murad, tells his story:[7]

> I accepted Jesus Christ in 2003. Then my wife, son, and daughter too put their faith in Isa (Jesus). And we committed ourselves to work for the kingdom of God. But we realized that to be effective and efficient for his kingdom, we needed to be enriched with biblical knowledge. We prayed to God that he may show us the way to know more about God's word and his plans for us. He answered that prayer by introducing me to SKT.

As pastors learn to share the word of God better, so believers are blessed in their relationship with God. But people also live among other people and have connections in society. TEE is working on these levels too. Rezaul is a believer who came to Christ through reading a Bible he found:[8]

> By reading the Book eagerly and carefully I accepted Isa Masih as my Savior. After this happened, I joined a TEE group of which I am still an active participant. Many thanks to God that he has given me the opportunity to complete eight courses already: Come Follow Me, Abundant Light, Christian Family Life, and the four books of The Life of Christ. At present I'm going into the fifth book of The Life of Christ series. I like the courses very much. I and others have benefitted from it. Christian Family Life is my favorite course. This has helped me to understand God's plans for us: to obey him as husband and wife, conjugal intimacy, and the roles of husband and wife in the family. I like all these. I especially like the chapter on forgiveness that showed me what forgiveness actually is and how we should forgive. I have already applied many of these in my personal life and in the society where I live. This has given me good results, and I expect more good fruits from it. The more

---

6. The content in this section was shared by Siebe Meindertsma at the Increase conference "Empowering Churches, Equipping Disciples," Chiang Mai, 13–17 November 2017.
7. His name has been changed for security reasons.
8. His name has been changed for security reasons.

we apply these courses to our lives, the more we will benefit from it. These are indeed life building courses.

Education Is Key

A growing church creates challenges. A pastor from Bangladesh Baptist Church Songho, John Sagar Karmakar, is also a tutor:

> In my church denomination, we have over 370 churches, and within these churches, we have almost a thousand people studying TEE in around forty groups. I am currently pastoring two churches on Sundays, and I also lead two TEE groups of primarily business and highly influential people. As pastors are not well paid in Bangladesh, young people are not interested in being pastors. Meanwhile, as the congregation of our city churches are made up of educated people, we need educated pastors. I see TEE as a tool to raise another generation of pastors. I have been blessed by TEE, and I would now like to challenge the younger people to be pastors through the TEE program.[9]

Bangladesh and Increase

One of the initial workshops of the Course Writers' Training was hosted by CCTB (see chapter 30), and several faculty members participated. Writers from CCTB are now developing new TEE courses for their context as a result. CCTB has given permission for two people, Wailes Rangsa, Director of Academics, and TEE Area Dean Siebe Meindertsma, to give some time as Increase Equippers; Wailes has been part of the Course Writers' Training, and Siebe is especially helping encourage growth of TEE in Myanmar. He was also a member of the 2017 Conference Planning Group. Shahidur Rahman,

---

9. John Sagar Karmakar, Increase conference "Empowering Churches, Equipping Disciples," Chiang Mai, 13–17 November 2017.

the Director of SKT, was also part of this planning group. Increase has held capacity building events at SKT.

Pray and Connect

Please pray
- for SKT, that they may continue to equip pastors and potential leaders effectively through TEE;
- that SKT may provide the necessary help to traditional leaders and pastors who have recently joined Agape and TEE activities, that they may work effectively among Muslim background believers in Bangladesh;
- for relationships with other institutions and mutual partnerships for the glory of God;
- for necessary resources (money, materials, laborers) to do the work in his kingdom.

CCTB is grateful to God for his leadership and mighty care over the past fifty years. They ask you to join their prayers for God's provision, guidance, and support over the next fifty years.

College of Christian Theology Bangladesh:
Facebook: https://www.facebook.com/CCTB-119784934708036/
General enquiries: cctbangladesh@gmail.com

Shikkha Kalyan Trust:
Contact address: SKT, P.O. Box-2, Gazipur-1700 Bangladesh
General enquiries: sktrust@outlook.com

MONGOLIA

9

Mongolia
A New Identity in Christ

Graham Aylett

Background[1]

Mongolia is a huge country with vast stretches of empty steppes where settlements are few and far between. Of the three million inhabitants, almost half live in Ulaanbaatar, the capital, while about 30 percent live a nomadic or semi-nomadic life. Just over half the population are Buddhists, while almost 40 percent call themselves non-religious. Most people in the country are of Mongol ethnicity. However, minorities such as Kazakhs, Tuvans, and others also live in Mongolia. Only around 2 percent described themselves as Christians in the 2010 census.

Mongolia's economy is traditionally based on herding and agriculture. Mining and heavy industry now also contribute. The economy is growing, but the proportion of the population below the poverty line was still around 30 percent in 2016. Alcohol abuse is a fact of life throughout Mongolian society.

---

1. The information in this section is from "Mongolia," Wikipedia, https://en.wikipedia.org/wiki/Mongolia.

TEE in Mongolia

The Mongolian church today is a young church. Although there were Mongolian Christians in the days of the great Khans, the modern Mongolian church celebrated its twentieth anniversary in 2012. There is a continuing need for discipleship resources that help believers to gain a good foundation of faith in their lives. There are also ongoing needs for leadership training resources. Learning to live, and learning to lead, under the Lordship of Christ is a process that requires profound changes in worldview.

Transformed Lives

Today at any given time, there are about six hundred TEE students throughout Mongolia, studying at foundation, certificate, and diploma level.[2] Abundant Life, SEAN's foundation level course for new believers, has been much used by God in Mongolia. Here are two examples:[3]

> From the first lesson of Abundant Life, my life became interesting. The weeks brought excitement, remorse, tears, joy. When in the second lesson we studied repentance, I asked my older brother for forgiveness. Before I was a believer, I had beaten him a lot, and he had really suffered because of my alcoholism. I came to understand that this was all wrong and found forgiveness both from God and from my brother. Because of this my brother was also saved. (Z., Hovd province)

> A whole new turnaround and change came about. I stopped drinking and smoking. I had been facing the threat of immediate imprisonment for any further disturbances of the peace. But now, I've become God's son, received eternal life, and have the Lord's love, and the Lord is changing and transforming me. This course has helped me understand that I am fully forgiven. (A., Arhangai province)

---

2. Hugh Kemp, "Remembering Mongolia," *GO magazine*, July 2015.
3. Both sent to Mongolia TEE; translated by the author.

TEE is a wonderful tool for groups of believers scattered in remote places. The church is built up through this training. One example is a church in the province of South Gobi, an area which is larger than Bangladesh but has a population of just over sixty thousand. One church in the provincial center has planted churches all through the province. Back in 2011, Pastor Natsagdorj shared,

> We have used TEE materials from 2002 onwards. All the daughter churches we planted also see TEE as a key part of the ministry, and all the church planters we sent out have been trained as group leaders. We see that leading Abundant Life and Abundant Light brings people together in a group for discussion and fellowship. This ministry has become a means of getting a church going.[4]

Equipping Disciples

Mongolia TEE (MTEE) was founded in 1995. In 1996, the very first TEE group was formed. Several of the original group members continue to use TEE courses, and one is now working among Buryat Mongols in southern Russia. By 2015, "a simple seed of an idea had grown to become a dynamic movement extending to the remotest nomad family in Mongolia's farthest provinces, equipping disciples throughout Mongolia's cities, and even penetrating into Mongolia's prisons,"[5] reflects Hugh Kemp, founder of Mongolia TEE and one of the first missionaries in Mongolia.

But Abundant Life and Abundant Light are just the beginning. Mongolia TEE developed a Certificate in Christian Ministry program to help train leaders – not only church leaders, but also people who could influence others around them in society. One church that used the certificate program was the House of Prayer, a new church planted in 2004 on the outskirts of the capital, Ulaanbaatar. The pastor, Lkhagvasuren, used the certificate program to train local elders and leaders, and numbers of them have gone on to lead churches

---

4. Ts. Natsagdorj, to the Mongolia TEE Users' Forum, Ulaanbaatar, 26 April 2011. Translated by the author.
5. Kemp, "Remembering Mongolia."

themselves. One of them was Ganchimeg. After finishing the program, she shared that, "The certificate level program has prepared my heart for mission, has encouraged me, and is a wonderful training."[6] Although a single woman, she went to a remote settlement in the Mongolian countryside, set up using her professional skill as a hairdresser, gossiped the gospel as she snipped hair, and planted a small house church there.

Another church using the certificate program was the Jesus Assembly in Erdenet. After completing the program, a group of graduates received permission to start TEE classes in a high-security prison. God moved. Prisoners came to Christ. One of them who had tried to take his life many times was completely changed: "Now I am at peace and filled with happiness. I praise my Lord God that I am no longer the man that I used to be, but that he has made me into a new man!"[7]

The certificate program can be run in groups at one church. But starting in 2010, MTEE invited people from different churches to come together for small groups meeting weekly in the MTEE office. Having members of different local churches meet and share in one small group has proved beneficial: they learn from one another, are encouraged, experience unity in prayer, and can share about problems in their local churches and try to find solutions together. These "mixed" groups have spread, and now there are some 240 students in over thirty groups, with three quarters of them in the countryside.

Mongolia TEE already serves Mongolians in the US, several European countries, and South Korea and has a vision to develop this diaspora ministry. They also work together with Increase. Mongolia TEE hosted one of the initial workshops of the Increase Course Writers' Training (see chapter 30). As a result, a team from Mongolia TEE are developing a new TEE course on the spirit world for their context.

---

6. T. Ganchimeg, from her testimony at her graduation, February 2009. Translated by the author.

7. As reported to Mongolia TEE. Translated by Simon Monster.

Holistic Leadership Training: The Kingdom Leadership Training Center

There is another, independent training center that uses TEE methodology and Mongolia TEE materials, the Kingdom Leadership Training Center (KLTC). KLTC was launched in 2009 after research into the Mongolian context and needs for leadership training. KLTC uses Mongolia TEE courses and other materials, but in a very carefully designed framework created by focusing on the needs of the students and outcomes that the Center wants to see in students' lives and ministries. The result is a program that obviously "scratches where it itches."

For example, Baagii was taking on the responsibility for leading his church when the pastor went abroad for study. He said, "We are not learning things we don't use. That is the exciting thing to me. What we learn, we use!" Otgoo, another church leader, said, "I'm involved in church leadership, and I can apply what I'm learning straight away. It is very practical." The students' personal spiritual growth is intentionally integrated into the different courses, rather than as a number of additional activities or courses. Deegii runs a day-care center where parents pay to leave their pre-school children when they are both out at work. She comments, "Every day, the home studies help to build up our relationship with God." Erika comments, "KLTC has challenged and encouraged growth in my personal life, not just academically. Through KLTC, I am learning how to be a better servant in the local church, and a better wife and mother."[8]

These students are examples of the holistic growth that KLTC is aiming for – not only growth in head knowledge, but learning in the areas of knowing, being, doing, and relating. One of the faculty at KLTC is Tuya, the Academic Coordinator. She became a believer through the testimony of her brother and knows God has used her life experiences to lead her into this role.

> When I was seventeen, an American missionary couple offered me the job of housekeeper during the day and the opportunity to attend Bible study at night. My father was unhappy about it, as serving foreigners meant "losing face." We avoided each

---

8. From interviews as part of an evaluation visit, March 2016.

other for a while, but when my father read the Bible himself, his attitude changed, and he gave me his blessing. In my years as a housekeeper, I learned English through speaking and listening.[9]

Encouraged by her pastor, Tuya went to serve on the Doulos ship for two years. While she was on the ship, she understood that "God's purpose for my life is to serve in his kingdom. I started to see how he had put people in my life to teach me English and train me in biblical knowledge." Returning to Mongolia, she married and became a mother. She also got job offers for translation and accepted the one in the Leadership Training Center. "While I worked, I also obtained a degree in English from a local university in 2013." Following Jesus has been a fruitful journey.

I also see fruits in my family. He has blessed me with a husband who loves God and our three adorable children. Many of my family members – my mother, sister, nephews, and nieces have also come to know the Lord, and some are serving him on the mission field. God gives me the gift of English to work with people of other nationalities. He put many people in my life to teach, guide, and demonstrate his love for me. How could I be currently working on improving Christian leadership programs at certificate, diploma, and degree levels for my people without those influences? In Christ, I have found my new identity.[10]

As believers like Tuya receive their new identity in Christ, they build on it and pass it on to others.

---

9. Tuya, "God gave me English to serve him," interview by ML Low, November 2017.

10. Tuya, "God gave me English to serve him" interview.

Pray and Connect

Please pray

- for Mongolia TEE and KLTC as they work together to prepare more courses at the foundation level;
- that these courses would serve the great majority of Mongolian believers, and also provide a better transition for those called to leadership;
- for Mongolia TEE to develop better support and training for group leaders, to open further "mixed church" groups, and to reach out to more Mongolians in the diaspora around the world;
- for the Mongolia TEE staff who are working on a new course on the spirit world especially for the Mongolian context, as part of the Increase Course Writers' Training course;
- for the long-term sustainability of KLTC, offering effective, fruitful, and affordable programs;
- for the process of transition to Mongolian leadership at KLTC over the next five years.

Mongolia TEE
YouTube: "Mongolia TEE Introduction" (three part documentary): https://www.youtube.com/watch?v=isqHhfJcTPY; https://www.youtube.com/watch?v=01sRO3WLWCM; https://www.youtube.com/watch?v=EnWycbp8QSY

Kingdom Leadership Training Center
General enquiries: Mark Wood, mark@mongoliawoods.com
Facebook: https://www.facebook.com/cltcmongolgmailcom

ZAYA'S STORY
with Penelope Vinden

© ML Low

When I was at Bible college in Mongolia, I was praying for a job that would use what I had learned. There are very few Christian jobs in my country, so I knew it would be difficult. I looked and looked and found one as a book editor! I didn't really know what I would be doing, but I took the job. So for six years I have worked with the TEE program editing courses, doing design, and redoing the commentaries because of a new translation of the Mongolian Bible.

I am also adapting a course on spiritual warfare that was written in the Philippines. It was written for their culture, and I am contextualizing it for our own culture. As Mongolians, we have many old traditions in our background. The culture in the Philippines seems to be interested in angels, but we aren't – we are only concerned with spirits. And the biggest influence on our ideas of spirits is shamanism. We also have influences from communism, Buddhism, atheism . . . and many believers communicate with God but still hold on to other non-Christian beliefs as well.

I think the most difficult thing Christians face is confronting their Buddhist or shamanist worldview. Their family, their friends, the whole culture is against the Bible. When people become Christians, they always say, "Oh, I can't do this and that, but I can do this." They want to make rules. So I have to push them a little and say, "It is more than rules!"

The first generation of Christians are struggling to develop a biblical worldview. Who is God? How do we communicate with him? Most people think God is someone we have to please. Someone far away. We have a lot to learn! But with TEE, step by step we gain knowledge.

I've really been encouraged over the past six years by a verse written by Paul about his ministry. In Ephesians 3:8, he says that he is the least of all God's people, but God gives him grace to preach. God gave me this ministry because I am faithful. I'm not doing this work for myself but for the next generation. This makes me stronger and gives me more joy.

I'm very happy that God called me to this ministry and very honored, too. I see Mongolians – of my generation, older, the ones just growing up – and I think, *There are so many things to do for them!*

CENTRAL ASIA

10

Central Asia 1
The Parched Land
Will Be Glad

Hanna-Ruth van Wingerden

Background[1]

Central Asia is an intriguing, mysterious, and little known part of the world to many people. It is comprised of Kazakhstan, Kyrgyzstan, Uzbekistan, Tajikistan, Turkmenistan, and Azerbaijan. In this section, we will refer to Central Asia in general and not to particular countries, because not all of these countries are free and safe places for Christians. Although each country is different and faces its own special challenges, they also share values and cultures, partly because all of these countries were part of the Soviet Union until 1991, partly because many are on the Silk Road, and partly because they were mostly Muslim regions before they became part of the Soviet Union.

Under Soviet rule, people groups in Central Asia were often moved to live in different areas than where they were originally from. This resulted in a melting pot of ethnicities. Each country has a number of people groups. For

---

1. The information in this section is from "Central Asia," Wikipedia, https://en.wikipedia.org/wiki/Central_Asia accessed July 2018; "Kazakhstan," Wikipedia, https://en.wikipedia.org/wiki/Kazakhstan, accessed July 2018; and "Uighurs," Wikipedia, https://en.wikipedia.org/wiki/Uighurs, accessed July 2018.

example, Kazakhs don't just live in Kazakhstan, but also in the surrounding countries, and Tajiks live in Uzbekistan, Kyrgyzstan, and Kazakhstan as well as Tajikistan. Uighurs are spread among the countries in Central Asia and China and do not have their own country. While the relevant ethnic group makes up the majority in each Central Asian country, Russians also make up a large percentage of each population, and Russian is still widely spoken, both of which have sometimes led to tensions.

The region is relatively stable politically. Most of the countries are under the strong rule of elected presidents who have been in power for many years, some since 1991. Freedom is a relative term for people who have different views on politics, or who hold beliefs other than mainstream Islam. Religious freedom varies greatly. It is very restricted in Turkmenistan and Uzbekistan, while things are a little more relaxed in Kyrgyzstan. In the bigger cities, it is usually easier to be a Christian than it is in the countryside.

TEE in Central Asia[2]

One of the challenges for churches in Central Asia is discipling believers from a Muslim background. Many areas are quite poor, and health care organized in state hospitals is often not the best. Not a lot of people can afford private clinics. So apart from theological training, many teams are involved in ways of helping physically. They work and do TEE in rehabilitation centers for alcoholics, in hospitals, in tuberculosis hospitals, and among groups of disabled people.

Many people live outside the cities in the mountains of Kyrgyzstan and Tajikistan, on the outstretched steppes of Kazakhstan, or in tiny villages in the countryside of Uzbekistan and Turkmenistan. A pastor in one of these remote regions in Central Asia says: "Our church is based on small groups, and there has always been a need for good, sound material for small groups. We used many different programs, and there were some results. But as a pastor, I wanted something more."

In August 2016, this region was visited by a TEE team. They did a presentation of the TEE SEAN materials. The pastor was impressed:

---

2. Unless otherwise mentioned, the testimonies and stories in this chapter were communicated to the authors between 2012 and 2018.

The first thing that attracted me was that it included group discussion. I also appreciated the Bible-based topics. I decided to try this material in our church, and I saw remarkable results. The small groups revived. I see now how brothers and sisters share their opinions and are not afraid to ask questions. I could see potential group leaders who are faithful and able to teach others. Small groups became active and attractive; the church began to grow in numbers as well as spiritually. These courses are especially valuable for us, since we are in the distant region, and there is no possibility for believers to receive theological education.

Growing in Leadership

Another pastor said, "I'm leading small groups myself through weekly group meetings. By using TEE materials, I came to know our church members better. I know their pains. I know their needs. I know where they are in their spiritual journey. It gives me lots of thoughts and ideas what to preach about on Sundays."

John[3] studied TEE courses as part of the curriculum of a theological seminary, and he has also been greatly affected by the TEE courses:

> With God's help, I went through an entire two-year course of study and acquired many practical skills and biblical truths for my life in Christ. My house is open for services. Every week a small group meets in our house. I also teach other groups in different places. I thank God for this useful discipleship tool. It is really applicable in various contexts and cultures.

Planting Churches[4]

TEE is often part of the wider work of churches, and it is also used for mission and social care. One of the groups that uses TEE courses is studying in a

---

3. His name has been changed for security reasons.

4. This section is based on interviews with team members in Central Asia by Hanna-Ruth van Wingerden at the Increase conference "Empowering Churches, Equipping Disciples," Chiang Mai, 13–17 November 2017.

rehabilitation center for drug and alcohol addicts. The people in this center are very inspired by the fact that they can easily understand the materials. They see that through the studies, the word of God opens up more deeply and becomes more practical for them. It transforms their lives.

In one of the countries of Central Asia, a group of pastors from six churches has come up with a plan for mission in their own country, and TEE is part of this. The purpose of this plan is to plant new churches in rural areas. A group of pastors and church members travels to villages to tell people about Jesus with the intention of starting home churches in these villages. There has been one mission trip so far. One of the participants of this trip was a student who had completed the TEE studies.

When they arrived in one village, they reached out to a few families. They preached the gospel and prayed for the sick. When the mullah, the preacher in the local mosque, heard of this, he was not too happy. But the mullah was having problems with his feet, and he was in a lot of pain because of that. One of the pastors laid his hands on this man's feet and began to pray for him. This opened the heart of this leader. He thought it was so special that a stranger knelt before him to touch his feet, and he was very moved. In this country's culture, it is unusual to touch someone's feet. But because of this action, a heart was opened for the gospel. The mullah asked the group to come back soon and stay in his house.

One of the pastors said, "TEE is essential in doing mission work like this. For new churches in the rural areas, it is a very useful tool. The materials can be used even in places where no pastor or church leader is present. People can do the courses together and learn more about the word of God."[5] He loves that TEE is based completely on God's word and not on people's ideas. Time and time again he sees hearts and lives transformed. When people do Abundant Life, for example, they learn to see that God's word is not only relevant in church, it is relevant on any day and in every aspect of life.

---

5. Anonymous TEE team member in Uzbekistan, interview by Hanna-Ruth van Wingerden at the Increase conference "Empowering Churches, Equipping Disciples," Chiang Mai, 13–17 November 2017.

"God Saved Me from the Temptation to Steal at Work"

An example of how God uses these courses to change people's life, and not just their mind, is the story of Malika.[6] She shares, "I worked in a hospital as a storage keeper in the kitchen. Wages were not high, and therefore taking advantage of my position, I used to take some products home."

Malika was invited to church by a friend and became a believer. She then started the Abundant Life course and really enjoyed the group discussions and studying the Bible together.

> One day people of the Orthodox Church brought a lot of products to our hospital and distributed them to our patients. I thought about how much this would cost in the shops and that these were paid for by donations of believers. And when, once again, I wanted to put some food in my bag, the Lord spoke to me: *How can you steal from these people who are also creations of God?* From that day I stopped taking food from work.

When Malika continued the TEE course, she was touched by an illustration of a girl who said, "I thank God that he saved me from the temptation to steal at work." It struck her that this was about herself. Since that time, Malika's life has changed very much. Her health and her relationships at home have improved.

> I used to think that if I did not bring food from work, we would not have enough to feed our family. But now we live on our wages and sleep peacefully. I am grateful to God for the writer of the course Abundant Life, which impacted my life so much. Through this course, you can say I was born again. It helped me to grow in faith.

Malika keeps studying courses, and she is now also a group leader who is impacting others in her church.

---

6. Her name has been changed for security reasons.

Pray and Connect

Please pray

- for churches and believers in remote regions to feel connected to other Christians;
- for the TEE programs working in Central Asia in difficult circumstances under a lot of spiritual pressure.

The Vision Group for Central Asia prays for and supports the teams in this region.

General enquiries and to subscribe to prayer letters: centralasia@gzb.nl

11

Central Asia 2
Investing in Young Believers

Hanna-Ruth van Wingerden

Background

The previous chapter shows how TEE is expanding in Central Asia. Kyrgyzstan was the first country with a national TEE movement that started in 2006. Increase, with others, brought together church leaders from Central Asian countries for a TEE workshop in 2012. As a result, new national TEE programs in the other republics, Uzbekistan, Tajikistan, Kazakhstan and Turkmenistan, were established. One of these programs now gives support for two of the team to serve more widely as Increase Equippers. In Azerbaijan, TEE has also been introduced, but there is no national movement as of yet.

Since those first years, the teams have seen tremendous growth. The latest figures show that ninety-four churches throughout the region are actively using TEE courses. Compared to eighteen months previously, this is an increase of more than 10 percent. The number of active students is even more remarkable. At the moment over 2,200 students are actively participating in TEE courses in 316 groups. This is a growth of 76 percent compared to 2016. That means that within participating churches, more people are receiving solid biblical training.[1]

---

1. Richard Brown, "Theological Education by Extension in Central Asia: An Evaluation of Recent Trends and Future Trajectories through the Lens of the Religious Markets Theory," unpublished paper, 2007.

With this growth comes many challenges and questions that need to be addressed. One of these challenges is the need for ongoing discipleship within churches where most members are first-generation believers from a Muslim background. How can TEE provide courses that are relevant for the people in Central Asia and the challenges they face as Christians? This story is about meeting those needs.

New TEE Courses for First-Generation Believers[2]

Alysa and Katarina are both from Central Asia.[3] They are part of an exciting new initiative launched by the Increase Association to train a new generation of TEE course writers in Asia for Asians. You can read more about this initiative in chapter 30. Alysa and Katarina are surrounded by others who support them with prayer, proofreading, and other practical matters. The training has been provided through a series of three workshops spread over a year and a half, and they have the ongoing support of an experienced mentor. The team in Kyrgyzstan hosted one of the initial workshops for Increase. Two teams are writing courses in and for Central Asia.

When Alysa and Katarina looked at their context, one thing specifically grabbed their attention. They realized that there were many young people in the churches! And almost every one of these young people was the first in their families to follow Jesus – they were nearly all first-generation believers. So they had no Christian parents or other Christian relatives to teach them the ways of the Lord, and they had no models of what it means to lead a Christian life.

An example of a first-generation believer in Central Asia is Aiman.[4] Aiman is a young assistant pastor in a church in Kyrgyzstan, and a member of the TEE team in his country. He first saw TEE in action when a pastor who was part of the TEE team met with him. The pastor told Aiman about faith in thoughts, words, and deeds, which had a huge impact on Aiman. After some time, he

---

2. This section is based on an interview by Hanna-Ruth van Wingerden at the Increase conference "Empowering Churches, Equipping Disciples," Chiang Mai, 13–17 November 2017.

3. Their names have been changed for security reasons.

4. His name has been changed for security reasons.

started to work through the foundation level TEE course, Abundant Life. "The first lesson was amazing!" he says.

> My father died when I was just twelve years old. I spent a lot of time with my uncles and eldest cousins; they became my father figures. One of them received Jesus, and he would always tell me about him. I got bored with his many visits and evangelizing. One time I pretended to receive Jesus before him because I was annoyed and hoped he would leave me alone. I also did it because I didn't want him to treat me harshly as he sometimes used to do before he became a believer.
>
> This decision, to receive Jesus just for my cousin, weighed heavily on my conscience for a very long time. I didn't just lie to my cousin and myself, but to God personally. This problem pressed me down for more than ten years, even when I served in a church in a youth ministry, because I was not sure about my salvation. But after the first lesson, I understood that I am a child of God, I belong to him, and nobody and nothing can ever take me from his family. That took away my fear.[5]

In his TEE ministry, Aiman is now involved in printing materials and distributing them to the groups that need them. Besides that, he is taking care of the design and technology side of things. Most importantly, he trains new TEE group leaders. "I love seeing how TEE builds a strong foundation of faith in believers. Pastors learn to use the word of God every day; they learn to be a disciple every day." Aiman goes on to explain that TEE is a good tool to get deeply into God's word and to train yourself in your daily life. "TEE lessons help you understand how you can be guided by the Holy Spirit in your normal, everyday life and to show Christ to your family, friends, neighbors, church, and community. And it is amazing to see the growth and change in people." The TEE program has had a huge impact on churches and people who are taught by pastors following the courses.

---

5. Aiman is a team member from a Central Asian TEE team who was interviewed by Hanna-Ruth van Wingerden at the Increase conference "Empowering Churches, Equipping Disciples," Chiang Mai, 13–17 November 2017.

Investing in Young People

One of Aiman's desires is for young people to give their heart to Christ. "It is important that they learn to be a real disciple of Christ when they are young, so that they don't live their lives in the ways of the world, but according to God's truth, full of wisdom and strength." Aiman leads a group of young teenagers. He finds it amazing to see their faith as strong as a rock. He says, "They really apply the lessons in the course to everyday life. In that way it is not just me teaching them; they also teach me. So we grow closer to God together."

Alysa, Katarina, and Aiman share the same vision and hope for young people to be discipled by their local churches. For first-generation believers, discipleship won't happen in their families! In fact, many young people in Central Asia, especially in the poorer regions, may have no parental example at all. As many adults seek employment in other countries like Russia and Kazakhstan, they are forced to leave their children behind, sometimes in the care of grandparents or an older sibling. This means that many children are growing up without parents. How can you learn to be part of a family, let alone a Christian family, if you have no one to show you?

Both Alysa and Katarina get many questions from young people about Christian behavior and lifestyle. So when they were thinking about writing a new course, the needs of these young people came to their minds. They believed a course on pre-marital relationships would be very helpful. The course fits well within their wider aim of discipleship and lifelong learning. The aim of discipleship is to build strong believers who can go on to build strong Christian families. This course offers a first step towards growing healthy Christian families. If people can learn how to have good relationships with others, later on they will be better equipped to build a strong family and raise their children as Christians, which will help to strengthen the future of the church. This course is not meant to stand alone; the two writers see it as the first step in a series on the topics of family life and marital relationships.

Growing in Christ

Something, perhaps unexpected, that Alysa and Katarina have found through writing this course is that God has used it for their own personal growth. Alysa said she used to be very nervous when people asked her questions and was afraid she wouldn't be able to answer. But God is teaching her that having all the right answers is not what it is about. What matters is that you are able to ask the right questions, questions which help you and others learn and grow. "I need to learn to ask the right questions. The course writing is helping me to do this," she says. Katarina agrees that she is growing through writing this course. She has found that when she is doing the work of God, she sees that God is working in her. She works to help others, and through that he changes her heart and mind, and he is growing his will in her life.

Alysa and Katarina desire that the course they are writing in Russian will be translated into other Central Asian languages. And they hope that more people will write courses specifically for Central Asia so the church in this region will grow.

Pray and Connect

Please pray

- for Alyssa and Katarina as they write their course, for God's protection, and that they stay strong in the Lord. They see that the devil is trying to destroy God's plans;
- for young people like Aiman and the teenagers he serves, that they may become a generation of believers through which Christ grows his church.

The *Vision Group for Central Asia* prays for and supports the teams in this region.

General enquiries: centralasia@gzb.nl

ADIL'S STORY[6]

with ML Low

I worked as a Muslim imam (religious leader) in a mosque from age twenty-seven to thirty. During one Ramadan (fasting) month, I involuntarily proclaimed, "Jesus is the Lord!" three times. I tried to fight this, saying, "No, Jesus is a prophet, not the Lord." I asked Allah, "What does this mean?"

A small, gentle voice answered, "It is the secret of God." I was totally confused. My behavior and attitude changed quite drastically. I did not understand what was happening to me. People could not understand me. Many thought I was crazy. I went to the church to look for my friend who had once shared the gospel with me. In the church I heard people singing worship songs. I did not think it was right to worship in songs. I wanted to leave but could not walk out of the church, so I stayed on.

For the next six months, I would go to the mosque every Friday for the preaching and to the church every Sunday for the sermons. I read the Quran and the Bible to compare them and find the truth. One Friday, when I was at the mosque at lunch time for prayers, I could not control myself. I cried all afternoon till evening.

I also had a lot of dreams and experienced many miracles in my life. I challenged Jesus, "If you are a living prophet, give me a sign." I then saw a light coming down from heaven. I asked this light, "Are you Jesus?" and the light responded by moving upwards.

On 9 September 2000, I said, "Jesus, please come inside me and change me." And he did. After accepting Jesus, I started to love people, including Russians whom I had always hated.

In those days, I worked in construction. One Sunday at church, I gave all of my last five coins in the offering. The next day when I went to work, the project owner gave me more money than I deserved and also more than what

---

6. His name has been changed for security reasons.

my supervisor would get. I asked the owner, "What am I to do with the extra money?" I thought it should go to my supervisor.

But the owner said, "The money is only for you." I was very surprised, and I knew then it was from Jesus.

I enrolled at a Bible school for three years, then tried to plant house churches. I once had twenty-five new believers, but as I did not know how to disciple them, gradually they all left to join other churches. Shortly after I met someone who invited me to a presentation on TEE at a Bible college. Nearly everyone else there rejected TEE, but I saw just what I needed! KuCH-TEE, the first TEE national team in Central Asia, was formed in November 2006. "KuCH" means power to serve.

TEE courses are reaching even the most remote places

Discipling the Diaspora

The term "diaspora," which literally means "scattering," describes people who move to another country in search of work, education, or refuge. Among them are many Asian Christians scattered within and beyond Asia. TEE enables these diaspora Asians to create discipleship groups in their own heart languages, sustains their spiritual growth, and supports their witness to fellow migrants. This section includes four examples of how TEE helps diaspora Asians in practice.

CENTRAL ASIA

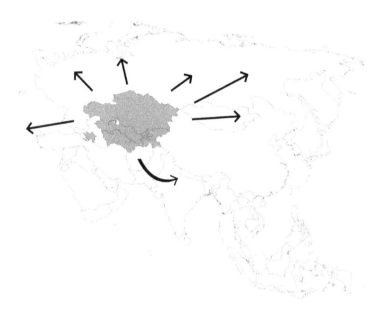

12

Central Asia 3
Migrant Mission

Hanna-Ruth van Wingerden

A Mix of People in Post-Soviet Countries

In the times of the Soviet Union, the countries in this union were quite closely linked. Due to voluntary and involuntary moves, Russian and other European people spread out over Central Asia, and people groups in Central Asia were forced to live in different countries. In many of these countries, Russian people still make up large chunks of the population. Besides ethnic Kazakhs, Kyrgyz, Uzbeks, Tajiks, and Turkmen people, many other people groups and minorities are still living side by side.

Although life in Central Asia is mostly peaceful, this mix of ethnicities creates challenges. Whereas Russians are considered Orthodox Christian, most Central Asians view themselves as Muslim. It is therefore problematic to change religion, as it feels like a betrayal of one's ancestry and identity. In addition, not every people group has the same opportunities and access to education and good jobs.

In many countries in Central Asia, Christians are not free because governments often regard them as members of sects that might disturb the status quo. These governments are keen to avoid giving space to extremist groups, and Christians are sometimes unjustly seen as such.

The demand for jobs in Central Asia is much higher than the supply. This means that laborers often go to Russia to earn income for their families. Since Russian is widely spoken in Central Asia, there are no language barriers, and travelling within the former Soviet Union is relatively easy, which makes Russia an attractive destination. However, working conditions are poor, and the attitude towards labor migrants is often negative because these people are seen as a source of problems for the Russian economy. All the more so as the economy is in decline due partly to Western sanctions.[1]

TEE for Central Asian Migrants in Russia[2]

In the east of Russia, a couple is working among Central Asian migrants using TEE courses. They themselves are from one of the countries in Central Asia.[3] The man, Ben, had a difficult youth and ended up in prison. But he became a believer, and his life changed. His family was against his conversion, but they saw they could not change his mind.

The woman, Una, had a good education and was a top student. She was very unhappy with her life as a man's third wife with two children to support, and she looked for answers in the Quran. This book showed her the problems in her life, but it didn't offer a solution, so she despaired. Later she heard about Jesus from a neighbor, and she knew he was the answer she had been looking for. Her marriage also ended and later she married Ben.

Ben and Una now work with labor migrants in their city. Una explains why they are working and investing in migrants, a group that everyone looks down upon. "These people have no rights, no status, no security, and are often ill-treated. No one cares about these people, so we have to," they explain. At first, they did not want to work with these labor migrants at all. But when they asked God how he wanted them to serve, they started noticing migrants. They

---

1. Douglas Green, "Labour migrants from Kyrgyzstan, Tajikistan and Uzbekistan to Russia amidst uncertain trends," *Stratfor*, 6 September 2017.

2. This section is based on an interview with two TEE workers from Russia by Hanna-Ruth van Wingerden at the Increase conference "Empowering Churches, Equipping Disciples," Chiang Mai, 13–17 November 2017.

3. Their names have been changed for security reasons.

saw how rooted in occultism they are and how hard their lives are due to the long working hours and the absence of family.

The couple use TEE materials to serve the migrants because the courses are so easy to understand and because they are a helpful discipleship tool. Many of the migrants they encounter have very basic or no education. But there are examples of people who have learned to read and write through the TEE courses! The fact that the materials are available in different languages helps a lot. People of different ethnicities can study together in groups because everyone can study and do homework in their own language and then meet for group discussions in Russian. The materials offer the opportunity for discipleship. After accepting Jesus, there is a real need to learn to follow him and to understand the Bible.

Ben comments that it is not easy at all for migrants from Central Asia to accept Jesus. The Islam in which they were brought up strongly holds them back from accepting Jesus. Another struggle is their reluctance to open up because their main motive for coming to Russia is to earn money.

One of the migrants Ben and Una met is a woman who works in a shop. She became a Christian through their conversations, and she wanted to study TEE. The only problem was . . . when to do it? After work she was too tired, so the only thing for it was to sit with her during working hours. In between serving customers, they would study and pray together. Then her employer found out and told her she was not allowed to stop working, even if there were no customers. Now they are looking for an opportunity to meet again, but this time is very hard to find. This woman's story is not unique: it is the same for most migrants who are working long hours without any days off.

TEE for Central Asian Migrants in South Korea[4]

People from Central Asia have not only moved into Russia, but also other countries. Russian-speaking ethnic Koreans, who settled in Siberia in the nineteenth century and were later deported to Central Asia by the Soviets, started to arrive in Korea soon after the collapse of the Soviet Union. Many

---

4. This section is based on personal communication to the authors from Pastor Dimitrii Hen, Suniy Church.

of them were from Uzbekistan. There are now about fifty thousand of these Russian-speaking Koreans and over twenty thousand Russian speakers of other nationalities in Korea. A large percentage of them are labor migrants who work in factories, in the agricultural sector, in food processing and packaging, and in other labor-intensive jobs.

There are about forty Russian-speaking churches in Korea, and some Korean churches serve Russian-speaking migrants as well. After the Increase conference in Asia in November 2017, several efforts aimed at starting up TEE among these churches started to come together and take shape. Pastor Dmitrii Hen from Suniy church was invited to the conference and met with many TEE workers. He got very excited about TEE and shared what he heard about TEE with other Russian-speaking pastors in Korea.

Pastor Hen invited the Uzbek and Russian team to run a training seminar for group leaders. The trainers first demonstrated a model lesson, and after that each participant had a chance to lead a group. During the seminar, the participants had wonderful group discussions – people opened their hearts and shared their life stories related to the group discussion themes and discussed practical application. Everyone seemed to get very excited about TEE. The unity and cooperation between the teams felt like a special blessing. Seventeen pastors and forty church members received certificates to become group leaders. In January 2018, the first TEE group started in Suniy church in South Korea.

Looking Ahead

The needs of migrants in any country are great. They are often overworked and very lonely. However for many, their time away from home is an opportunity to meet Jesus. When they become believers, there is a need for churches to receive them well and disciple them.

One thing Ben and Una want to focus on is encouraging the churches in their area to join their work. Ben is planning to give seminars to local churches to explain how they can help migrants, how to build bridges between the church and the migrants, what a migrant's life looks like, and how the church can help. They hope that this effort will give them more opportunities to work with local churches for the benefit of more migrants. Another key development is a new guest house. Ben is building this himself! This house will be a place where they can safely meet people and where migrants can sleep and eat and have a good place to do Bible study together.

Pray and Connect

Please pray

- for development, growth, and continuing unity in the TEE work in South Korea;
- for good fruit from the initial training sessions there and that the TEE courses will bless many Russian speakers in Korea;
- for Ben and Una to build lasting relationships with churches that will join them in migrant ministry;
- for migrants in other parts of Russia, particularly in Moscow, that God will provide ways to reach them.

The Vision Group for Central Asia prays for and supports the teams in this region.

General enquiries and to subscribe to prayer letters: centralasia@gzb.nl

HMONG

13

Hmong
Scattered in Diaspora

Graham Aylett and Hanna-Ruth van Wingerden

Background[1]

The Hmong are truly a people group in diaspora. Since the late eighteenth century, the Hmong have gradually left the southern provinces of China, where about 2.7 million still remain. Around 1.2 million of them have made the mountains of Vietnam, Laos, Thailand, and Myanmar their home. Over one hundred and seventy thousand Hmong now live in the United States and nearly twenty thousand in Europe. Australia, French Guyana, Canada, and Argentina are home to smaller groups of Hmong people.

In the twentieth century, the Hmong were caught up in conflicts in Southeast Asia, and many ended up in refugee camps. They were brought from there to safer countries including the United States, Canada, and France. Many families were broken up in the chaos, and many Hmong people are in an ongoing search to find their family roots and relatives in Asia.

The Hmong have a rich culture; they are known for their beautiful embroidery and love songs. Most Hmong people, both in Asia and the West,

---

1. The facts in this section are from "Hmong People," Wikipedia, https://en.wikipedia.org/wiki/Hmong_people; "Hmong," Encyclopaedia Britannica, https://www.britannica.com/topic/Hmong; and "Resources," Hmong District of Christian and Missionary Alliance, http://www.hmongdistrict.org.

still follow traditional spiritual practices that include shamanism and ancestor worship. Sickness and health are important themes in these beliefs. When someone is ill or has suffered bad luck, a shaman comes to the house. He then connects to the spirit world to heal the soul and through the soul the body of the patient. Missionaries have converted many Hmong people to Christianity since the nineteenth century, and many more have become Christians in the West.

Rooted in Biblical Teaching[2]

The Hmong Division of the Christian and Missionary Alliance in the USA has long made TEE a central element of its training program. Dr Jerry Yer Soung was co-founder of the TEE program in Thailand, and he has a vision for seeing Hmong Christians equipped as disciples of Jesus for mission and ministry.

The Hmong Ministerial Study Program (MSP) in the USA is the training program used by the Hmong Division of the Christian and Missionary Alliance in America, writes Carol Freeman, student pastor at Bethany Global University, Minnesota. SEAN's The Life of Christ is used as the main part of the first two years of their program. This means that all one thousand, three hundred students in their first and second year are studying SEAN and other TEE courses.

In July 2015, Carol attended a graduation and celebration of the thirtieth anniversary of the Hmong Christian Institute. It was a wonderful celebration with one thousand Hmong people present. The evening opened with a flag ceremony: five hundred students marched in and clustered around homemade identifying flags – one flag for each of their SEAN study groups. Many were wearing colorful Hmong attire. A pharmacist, who was one of the graduates, shared, "SEAN is simple but profound. I said I'd never go back to school. But I did. I'm glad I did because knowledge is not the same as relationship. SEAN materials gave me the backbone for what I believe."

The current Director of the Hmong Christian Institute is Pastor Lee Wang Chao. He says,

---

2. This section is based on an email from Carol Freeman, Bethany Global University, to Graham Aylett, 3 July 2015.

Twenty years ago, I was sent by my district, the Hmong C&MA district in the USA, to a remote village with a handful of Christians but no pastor or leaders. My role was to train leaders and then come back. A young couple lived in this village. They weren't Christians, but they asked me about my beliefs, and after sharing my faith, they received Christ. They enrolled in a TEE class and grew in faith. The TEE courses taught them how to grow in Christ, how to deal with issues such as temptation, and how to follow Jesus in daily life. They learned from the Master himself, from Jesus. Their faith was growing rapidly, and they were hungry to learn more. So they went to Bible college and came back to be pastors. The man is now a strong pastor. When I observe him and talk to him and the people he serves, I can really see that he has grown through TEE. He started with the right principles rooted in biblical teaching. It has been a very good resource for him.[3]

The Hmong Christian Institute continues to use TEE to train Hmong church leaders all over the world. The Institute is based in Colorado, and they give training in America and other countries. In some countries, they partner with other local organizations. These partnerships are especially helpful where other languages are spoken and local organizations can help to form a bridge.

Training Self-sustaining Leaders for the Local Church[4]

The Hmong Christian Institute hopes to be able to continue to provide more training to Hmong people, wherever they are. In the past, training was given in a "parachute" style: the team handed out materials, taught a course, and then left. However, recently they have been able to connect and build lasting relationships and partnerships with local associations. In Laos and Vietnam, the goal is to train potential leaders who are students. At first new students enroll and participate in the courses themselves. Then they are trained to be

3. Lee Wang Chao, shared at the Increase conference "Empowering Churches, Equipping Disciples," Chiang Mai, 13–17 November 2017.

4. Information in this section was shared at the Increase conference "Empowering Churches, Equipping Disciples," Chiang Mai, 13–17 November 2017.

group leaders. In the last phase of training, they are ready to lead groups while the Institute provides help only where needed. In this way, self-sustaining leaders are being trained for the local churches. The goal for 2019 is to train current students to become regional leaders who can take the work forward.

Serving Churches in Vietnam[5]

Dr Jerry Yer Soung knows that there are approximately 450,000 Hmong believers in the north of Vietnam. He is especially connected to a church alliance of more than a thousand churches that serves over 175,000 of the Hmong believers. A challenge for the work in this region is the variety of Hmong languages. As the Hmong people migrated to different parts of Southeast Asia, their languages started to differ. Some of the varieties are quite similar and widely spoken, and others are quite rare.

Most Hmong Christians in Vietnam speak and worship in a version of Hmong called Black Hmong; they don't use Vietnamese to worship God. While Blue and White Hmong are similar, Black Hmong is quite different. Dr Jerry Soung confesses he only understands a little bit of Black Hmong, which makes the work more difficult. Therefore, the Hmong District in America has adopted this people group as a project and are intending to create not only a new White and Blue translation of the courses, but also a Black Hmong translation. However, Black Hmong currently has no written language, so they are working with one of the Bible translation groups to get the language into written form.

Pray and Connect

Please pray
- for Lee Wang Chao and the Hmong Christian Institute, and for the many Hmong Christian leaders to be trained;
- for revision of the White and Blue Hmong TEE translations, and for the new Black Hmong translation;

---

5. This section is based on a conversation between Jerry Soung and Monty Winters, at that time Christian and Missionary Alliance Director for Ministry Studies, that was emailed to Terry Barratt in 2016.

- for effective use of TEE materials among Hmong believers wherever they are living.

Hmong District of the Christian and Missionary Alliance (USA):
Website: http://www.hmongdistrict.org
General enquiries: info@hmongdistrict.org

MALAYSIA

14

Malaysia
One Nation, Many Languages

Bob Teoh

Background

Like neighboring Indonesia, Malaysia is a Muslim majority country with a long history of Islam tracing back to the fifteenth century when it became firmly established. According to 2017 estimated figures, the total population of Malaysia is 31.4 million of which around 61 percent are Muslims and around 21 percent are Buddhists. Christianity comes a distant third at just over 9 percent, while around 6 percent of the population are Hindus. Two out of every three Christians in Malaysia are from the states of Sabah and Sarawak in Borneo and speak the Bahasa Malaysia language. A recent phenomenon is the growth of congregations of new believers from Malaysia's increasing migrant population, unofficially estimated at several million.[1]

Because of the many ethnic groups in Malaysia, it was natural for TEE to be developed in several languages at the same time. The work began within the last few years, as different streams bubbled up independently to serve different ethnic groups in their mother tongues. Now these streams are starting to flow together, so it is an exciting time for TEE in Malaysia.

---

1. "Malaysia," Wikipedia, https://en.wikipedia.org/wiki/Malaysia, accessed August 2018.

TEE in Chinese and English[2]

The story begins with a Korean-American couple, Pastor Shim and his wife, Jane, who introduced TEE to the Chinese-Americans Jason and Jane Lee.[3] You can read more about them in chapter 23. They in turn brought the Chinese language program to the Malaysia Baptist Theological Seminary in 2012. The seminary's Associate Dean, Dr Mooi Sai Lim, said,

> I wanted my students to study Bible courses in the Seminary which they could teach in the church. The Life of Christ course looked very simple, yet the knowledge is deep. . . . So I hope that all my first year students can attend this course as a base for the other Bible and theology classes. We are the first batch in Malaysia to take this course. Now we have many churches starting to teach this course.[4]

Albert Chai, a pioneering TEE enthusiast, encountered the six book The Life of Christ course through Jason and Jane and quickly introduced it in both English and Chinese to various churches in the country. One of these was the Anglican Church of the Good Shepherd in East Malaysia. Albert reported on what happened when its senior minister tried the training in his church:

> To his surprise, just after Book 1, he noticed a drastic change in how the leaders' team worked and in their enthusiasm in serving God. It has made his role as the senior pastor much easier. It has been three years since they started The Life of Christ. Their key leaders found that they can effectively build a stronger foundation for their new believers and facilitate the Abundant Life and Abundant Light courses with confidence and clarity. The archdeacon is recommending TEE to all his Anglican churches starting 2018.

---

2. Unless otherwise mentioned, the testimonies and stories in this chapter were communicated to TEE pioneers working in Malaysia.

3. Their names have been changed for security reasons.

4. Mooi San Lim, email to Graham Aylett.

Later in West Malaysia, Pastor Stephen Tang led a cohort of students through The Life of Christ. In Kuala Lumpur, another stream began when Increase Equippers gave training in Emmanuel Evangelical Free Church, and several people united their efforts to get TEE going in different urban congregations. TEE teaching proved acceptable in a range of denominations and churches.

The vison of Raymond Lee, then Interim Director, now Director of the national TEE organization, extends beyond the city. He is concerned about the migration of Christians to urban areas which leaves a vacuum of mature church leadership in the rural areas and small townships. TEE provides the ability to bring systematic theological training to these rural areas. Our recent effort to work with local churches has been very encouraging, with the students showing keen interest and spiritual hunger to learn the word of God.

In 2014, a serving base for the Increase Association was established in Malaysia. New opportunities to introduce Malaysian church leaders to TEE have arisen, and Increase has encouraged TEE ministry among different diaspora groups and the formation of a national umbrella TEE movement.

TEE in Nepali

Just one of the results of introducing TEE courses is the use of a new church planting model, particularly among new Nepali believers. Nearly a million people from Nepal work in Malaysia as security guards, factory workers, and restaurant workers. They work very long hours and hardly ever get a weekend off.

One young Nepali man was a Maoist back home. He joined the army but was later imprisoned. Somehow he ended up in Malaysia where he reluctantly attended an evangelistic meeting. God touched his heart, and the rest is history. He continued to work in Malaysia, and later he returned to Nepal where he married a Christian worker. They have planted four churches in Nepal since then and are discipling new believers. He says, "I am just doing what I learned in Malaysia."

The ministry among Nepalis started in 2002 when by divine appointment two young Christian Nepali workers, in their eagerness for fellowship, went to a church near them in Klang, not realizing that it was a Chinese-speaking church. The Chinese there directed them to a Tamil-speaking church nearby, not realizing they only spoke Nepali. Again by divine appointment, they were referred to Rina who speaks Hindi, a language related to Nepali. Rina and her husband, Martin, decided to take the Nepali Christians under their wings. The following Sunday, these two Nepalis invited two other Nepalis, and a fellowship was started for them. It grew to ten, to fifteen, and further multiplied to thirty, and they kept meeting regularly every Sunday. Rina and Martin felt compelled to start systematic discipleship with the Nepalis, but it was a challenge to find suitable resources for these new believers in their mother tongue.

Then in 2015, Rina and Martin encountered some sample TEE books in Nepali through Increase. By divine appointment, they were seated at dinner next to a board member of Increase who was also Director of the Institute of Theological Education by Extension Nepal (ITEEN). He immediately volunteered, "I will come personally to train your workers."

Actually, ITEEN had tried to start TEE groups in Malaysia before, but they couldn't keep going on their own. Once Martin and Rina gave their local support to the work, it started blossoming rapidly. Within three years, it grew to more than sixty TEE groups, with 380 students led by forty-two volunteer facilitators who are themselves Nepali migrant workers. The program was so successful and the TEE course books in such great demand that they are now printed in Malaysia. And when workers return to Nepal, they can continue their studies there. In 2018, the first national Nepali TEE conference was held to give thanks to God for this progress, to award certificates, and to appreciate publicly the volunteer group leaders.

TEE in Bahasa Indonesia and Malaysia

A missionary couple who were ministering to Indonesian domestic helpers first encountered TEE resources translated into the Bahasa Indonesia language through Increase. They thought the lessons were too simple but decided to give it a try. Then when they started, they found that they needed training to be able to use the materials well. So they attended the training workshop conducted by Graham and Nicola Aylett in Kuala Lumpur, where they understood how to use the course materials and the potential of TEE for discipleship.

As two thirds of the Christians in Malaysia speak Bahasa Malaysia, a focus group was formed to translate the TEE materials into that language instead of relying on Bahasa Indonesia. Despite the general similarity between the two languages, there are some significant differences. This translated material available in their mother tongue will strengthen Bahasa Malaysia-speaking Christians in their ability to defend their faith.

TEE in Other Languages

Due to the increasing presence of Pakistani Christians in Malaysia, many of them refugees, Pakistani pastor Rev Simon Patras launched some Urdu TEE groups using the courses from Pakistan. "This course has better equipped me, and through group discussions, it has boosted my confidence to share the gospel with others," testifies one student. "I hope and pray that just like me, many can benefit from this amazing Bible study program," says another. TEE helps to bring hope and confidence to refugees who are far from their homeland. TEE groups from Myanmar and other countries are also now growing gradually.

Moving Forward

An application is being submitted to the Malaysian authorities for the registration of a new national TEE organization with the provisional name of Systematic Theological Education Program (STEP).[5] The organization's interim chair, Raymond Lee, believes that TEE in Malaysia is steadily gaining ground in the effort to help local churches fulfill the Lord's Great Commission. He says, "We believe that TEE is for all Christians regardless of their denominational background and theology background. We find that it is vital to make sure that the churches in Malaysia are not only growing in quantity, but growing in quality, that it is mature and led by spiritual and well-trained leaders."

---

5. The situation has changed since this book was first published by Increase. STEP failed to register. However, the national TEE organization is now registered under another name: TEE Malaysia (TEEM).

Pray and Connect

Please pray
- for good relationships with the government and safe ways for the team to move forward;
- for wisdom in how to include the different language streams and for progress in translation projects.

General enquiries: Raymond Lee, raylee@pc.jaring.asia

First National Nepali TEE conference 2018
© ML Low. Used with permission.

DIASPORA

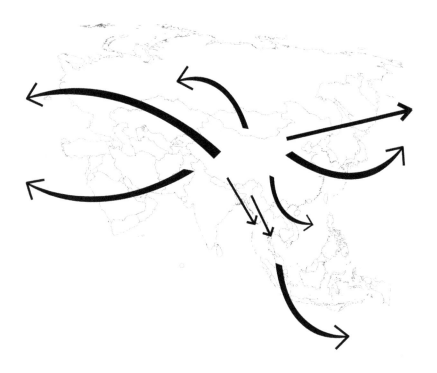

15

Diaspora
Discipling the Nations

Tim Green and Hanna-Ruth van Wingerden

Background

Millions of people in and from Asia live somewhere other than their homeland. Some of them, like the Hmong, have been scattered relatively recently for political reasons. Others, among them millions of Chinese, left the problems in their homeland long ago. Many people today relocate for economic reasons or to escape war or natural disasters. This chapter tells stories of how TEE is already being used among these diaspora communities in a range of surprising places. We will return to this topic in chapter 34 to think about wider implications and future opportunities.

Opportunities for the Gospel

In 2015, according to official UN statistics, 244 million people, or 3.3 percent of the world's population, lived outside their country of origin.[1] This situation creates a huge opportunity for the church to reach people who might not hear the good news otherwise.

---

1. "UN Migration Report 2015," United Nations, New York, 2016, https://www.un.org/en/development/desa/population/migration/publications/migrationreport/docs/MigrationReport2015_Highlights.pdf.

In fact, thousands of people are turning to Christ where they live in diaspora, as some of our other stories show. Diaspora churches are being planted across the world to serve the particular needs of believers who are outside their country of origin. Diaspora believers are sharing their faith with their diaspora community and are also returning to their home countries to share their faith with friends, family, and others.

For people in countries where the church is small, like Mongolia, relocating to another country provides a chance for them to hear the gospel when they are far from home. A Mongolian student in Austria shares,

> My name is Batjargal. I live and study in Salzburg. I was not a Christian believer in Mongolia. But having come to Austria, I met with Pastor Tugsuu, and I heard about Jesus from him. I received Jesus as my Savior. Then going through Abundant Life, I found out more about Jesus, and about the new birth, repentance from sin, faith and forgiveness, being obedient, and much more. It was a great time, a real blessing, and I grew in faith. And I learned a lot of Bible verses. Using the Bible verses I had memorized, I shared the good news with friends at school, and now two of them have started coming to church.[2]

TEE without Borders

In chapter 23, we tell the story of Jason and Jane Lee who work with Chinese churches in China and beyond. Chinese believers in Australia, Italy, Hong Kong, Hungary, Japan, Korea, Malaysia, Myanmar, Taiwan, the United Kingdom, the United States, and Vietnam are being trained using TEE.

Some of these Chinese TEE groups running outside of China are composed of students. One of the benefits of training these Chinese students as TEE group leaders is that after they graduate and return home to their homes in China, they can start running their own TEE courses. Previously Jason and Jane never had the human resources to reach all these parts of China, nor was it legal! Now with the help of TEE, so many more Chinese people are reached

---

2. Personal communication to the authors in 2018.

in an organic way, and many churches will benefit from leaders who have a solid theological grounding.

Diaspora TEE extends to more than the Chinese. For example, there are groups of Pakistanis studying in Malaysia and the Gulf countries. There are Russian-speaking immigrants in Turkey and Central Asian immigrants in Russia. TEE in the Khmer language first began in refugee camps where Cambodian Christians fled genocide. It followed some to their longer term home in the USA and others back into Cambodia after the war. There it grew, and recently, Cambodians sent TEE courses to New Zealand for a new group starting there. Diaspora TEE knows no boundaries.

Nepali TEE in Different Countries

Groups of Nepalis in India, Malaysia, the UK, and the US are being discipled with training and materials from ITEEN, the TEE program in Nepal. Its Director Tanka Subedi travelled to the UK in 2017 to visit ITEEN groups there. Throughout the UK, about one hundred students are doing the courses and growing in Christ. Among them are teenagers whose life is not always easy: they don't have a good community to relate to and can sometimes get into trouble. One of them said,

> I had some bad habits, but doing Abundant Life has changed some of them. I saw people my age discussing how to evangelize their friends, and buying chips and distributing them to people on the streets. Their lives were changing, and they were getting excited to do good works, showing the love of Jesus Christ to others.[3]

In Malaysia, at least 700,000 Nepalis work as security guards, factory workers, or other low paid jobs in bad working conditions.[4] The Christians among them are usually first-generation believers of Hindu background. Martin and Rina are a Malaysian couple who were looking for a way to disciple

---

3. Tanka Subedi at the Increase conference "Empowering Churches, Equipping Disciples," Chiang Mai, 13–17 November 2017.

4. "Nepalese People in Malaysia," Wikipedia, https://en.wikipedia.org/wiki/Nepalese_people_in_Malaysia, accessed July 2018.

these Nepalis in Malaysia in their mother tongue. Finally in 2015, the Increase Association helped them find an answer. ITEEN provided the material and training for the first group of Nepalis to start TEE in Malaysia. From there the discipleship just spread organically as Nepali believers were equipped through TEE discipleship groups and went on to start new groups. You can read more details in the previous chapter.

For example, one TEE student said the TEE courses have given him a way to understand God's word and to pass it on to others. When his contract finishes in Malaysia, he wants to return to Nepal where he plans to start discipleship groups through TEE in his own village.

Former Muslims Following Jesus

The TEE course Come Follow Me was written by Tim Green especially for followers of Christ from a Muslim background. It serves as an alternative to the widely used Abundant Life course, but especially tackles common issues faced by former Muslims. Come Follow Me was originally intended for users in a Muslim majority country, but soon it was picked up by diaspora believers far and wide. For example it helped a group of Afghan refugees in India who commented, "The strength of this book is that every brother and sister, young or old, has the opportunity to freely share their thoughts, questions, problems and pains – as they've experienced in their lives. It is this that makes the students interested and they open up and can pray, not for themselves but for others and have right understanding of Christianity."[5]

Tim has found that he can use the course even with those whose language he does not understand. For example with a group of Iranians, he prepares the self-study stage in English, and they do it in Farsi. The questions in the group discussions act as springboards from which the members dive into lively discussion in their own language. Of course, translation is sometimes necessary. But the group leader does not need to understand every word because members are learning from the book and from each other.

Until now the greatest use of Come Follow Me in Europe has been among Afghans, Iranians, and Arabs. So translations were needed for not only in

---

5. "What They Say," *Come Follow Me*, https://come-follow-me.org/about/what-they-say.

their own languages but also for German, French, and Norwegian, so that the Christians of those countries could use the course as a discipling tool. One German Christian leading a group commented,

> I, myself, am even a bit surprised how these become believers! They all attend my Come Follow Me course, and they have grown amazingly! I do think the course has helped these men to become real believers. Some of them say that they had told lies in their interviews in Sweden or Norway, and now they want to have a "new start" and tell the truth, even though it means that they will not get an asylum place here in Germany. They say it is better to have a clean conscience with God than stay in Germany because of lies![6]

Making It Work Practically

In 2015, the Increase Association set up a task group on diaspora TEE to follow its development and to see how it can best work in practice. By 2018, this group had gained enough experience to solve some key challenges. They found ways for printing to be done locally, for host country TEE organizations to support diaspora groups in their midst, and for group leaders to be trained locally.

Since the leaders live far from their country of origin, it is difficult and expensive to send someone to train them. However help is now at hand through a training package created by SEAN with help from Increase. This online resource enables four or five TEE leaders to come together face to face and practise the skills they need to lead group discussion. This package, which marks a breakthrough in group leader training, is available on https://connect. crosswired.com/web/c2927223. Increase also created a database of Asian TEE courses which is a great help for those in diaspora settings who want to know what is available in which languages.[7]

---

6. Email to Tim Green, 21 February 2018.
7. For available courses in Asian languages, see https://courses.increaseassociation.org/.

For Such a Time as This

God has sovereignly arranged for these TEE courses to be available in so many diaspora languages when people are on the move and "mixed up" as never before. These TEE courses can be used to disciple believers in their mother tongue wherever they are in the world! Wherever national churches have the vision to disciple people from other nations in their midst, we feel that TEE is poised to provide them with the tools they need. These tools were created for such a time as this.

Pray and Connect

Please pray

- for God to use this diaspora phenomenon to disciple many thousands of believers so they can grow strong in their faith and be active witnesses for Christ wherever God takes them;
- for wisdom for the Increase Task Group as they pioneer and support diaspora TEE as it develops in new countries;
- for good cooperation between the TEE programs so that TEE courses can be easily available, and for diaspora group leaders to have good training and support that can be sustained over many years to come.

General enquiries: increaseassociation@gmail.com

Available courses in Asian languages: https://courses.increaseassociation.org/

Christians under Pressure

Christians face increasing intolerance or even persecution in several parts of Asia today. This pressure may be fueled by political trends, nationalism, religious extremism, or often a toxic blend of them all. It can also be triggered when church growth becomes substantial enough to threaten the social status quo. In such circumstances, TEE can bring strength to Christ's followers and encourage them to persevere. Also, TEE groups are harder for governments to locate and close down than the more visible theological institutions. There are four chapters in this section, but countries like India, Russia, China, and those of Central Asia could easily have been added.

NEPAL

16

Nepal
Moving Mountains

Hanna-Ruth van Wingerden

Background[1]

Nepal is a small country in the Himalayas and is probably best known for its highest peak, Mount Everest. Around three quarters of the country is covered by mountains, and it has an estimated population of up to thirty million. Nepal is locked in between China and India, and the government tries to pursue an independent foreign policy. Due to its policy and geography, the country used to be very isolated and consequently is one of the least developed countries in the world. The economy depends on imports and money sent back by migrant workers. Most basic materials and consumer goods come from outside the borders.

Music and dance are very popular among Nepalese people. Drums and wind instruments have been used for centuries particularly in religious ceremonies, in which songs play an important role. Nepal does not have an official religion, but around 80 percent of the people are Hindu. Buddhism has also had a huge impact, and today about 10 percent of the people are Buddhist.

---

1. The facts in this section are from "Nepal," Wikipedia, accessed August 2018, https://en.wikipedia.org/wiki/Nepal; and "Nepal," Encyclopaedia Britannica, https://www.britannica.com/place/Nepal, accessed August 2018.

Nepal was closed to outside influence for a long time. When the British ruled over India, Nepal's Rana rulers made a deal with the British to keep their independence. In return for soldiers for the army, the Ranas were free to handle domestic affairs themselves. But when the British withdrew from India, the rulers in Nepal lost their support system, and after a few turbulent years, a democracy was born. This transition also opened up Nepal for the gospel. In 1952, a small group of medical missionaries walked across the Indian border and with the permission of the Nepali government set up a clinic in the Pokhara valley.[2]

TEE in Nepal

Nepal's church is less than seventy years old, but it has been one of the fastest growing churches in the world, despite facing persecution. Recently the government passed anti-conversion laws, and their implementation has added to the pressure. Even the constitution no longer allows people to change their religion. No one is allowed to share any religion apart from Sanatan or Hinduism with the intention to convert somebody. Practically this means that evangelism in any form is now completely against the law. Social work done by Christian NGOs is also becoming increasingly difficult. Church leaders met in Kathmandu in 2017 to discuss how to face this issue. With three hundred pastors in attendance, a new vision was formed to work towards a thousand new churches every year in the next five years. "They can stop us from going out, but they cannot stop people coming into the church!" said Tanka Subedi, Director of ITEEN.[3]

The Institute for Theological Education by Extension in Nepal (ITEEN) is the organization that provides TEE materials and courses in Nepal. ITEEN is playing a very important role in the growth of the church in these difficult circumstances. Using simple language, TEE courses are helping believers, even if they have minimal education, to learn about God and about doing ministry

---

2. "Our Story," International Nepal Fellowship, https://www.inf.org/about/our-story, accessed July 2018.
3. Tanka Subedi at the Increase conference "Empowering Churches, Equipping Disciples," Chiang Mai, 13–17 November 2017.

in the church. Currently there are over 6,800 active TEE students who are church members and leaders. Despite the restrictive laws, 1,079 new students enrolled in one of the courses, and over three hundred students graduated. Nepalis are also studying ITEEN courses in the Nepali diaspora around the world. You can read more about this topic in chapter 15.

ITEEN hosted the 2010 Increase conference, which was a wonderful service to Increase! The Director of ITEEN, Tanka Subedi, as well as being a member of the Increase Committee, is an Increase Equipper who has represented Increase at significant meetings in Thailand and India. Increase helped ITEEN with the preparation of a five-year strategic plan in 2014. One of the ITEEN team, ND Lama, is also an Increase Equipper, with special interest in the digital world.

TEE for Church Planting[4]

Course Development Coordinator for ITEEN, Rita Subedi, says, "TEE is bringing the church quality." There are many examples of how people have changed and how the churches are growing because of TEE, a few of which we will share here. One example of the power of God in ordinary people is the story of Ram Bahadur. As a young boy, he caught leprosy and became "untouchable." He had to leave home to get treatment, and as he was being treated, he heard the gospel and received Christ in his life. Ram never went to school, he doesn't have fingers, and he cannot speak proper Nepali, yet this man was chosen by God to plant churches. Ram says,

> I had a strong feeling that God was calling me to serve him as a pastor and a church planter. I started praying about it and talked about it with my pastor. After several talks I was anointed as a pastor in September 2008, together with other believers who were anointed as elders and deacons. Our church, "Mukti Mandali," was also inaugurated officially and started on that same day.

The only theological education Ram has is through ITEEN courses.

---

4. The information in this section is from the ITEEN Annual Report July 2013–July 2014.

I am very thankful to ITEEN because it has helped us in the growth of our church spiritually and practically. I have not attended any Bible schools and do not hold any academic degrees except for ITEEN. The courses have helped me to know the guidance of God and to commit myself to his calling and serve him.

Ram Bahadur planted seventeen churches in eight years between 2008 and 2016 in the remote hills of Nepal. He continues to see the need for TEE as a way to raise up leaders. "We are praying for more leaders because our churches are growing so rapidly in number, and if we cannot give them good education based on the Bible, our members will not be strong enough to live a rightful Christian life."

Once the churches are planted, ongoing training and support for local believers is essential. One church leader in a small village writes,

In villages, we do not get any training, and we are ministering empty-handed. We lead people with the encouragement that we received a long time ago when we first met with the Lord. As we do not get any training, we are draining away. I was very agitated. I was wondering how to lead all these people because we do not have anything to lean on. Then I decided to do this TEE course. When I did these two lessons for practical classes, I was very happy because I found what I have been praying for – a course which can be done at home to learn about God.

Stories of Change[5]

Udaya Lama shares how God changed his life through ITEEN.

My mother is a good Christian, and she used to encourage me a lot to go to church meetings. But I did not like it when someone told me about God. I was getting involved in a circle of bad friends and spiraling downwards. Even when I found a good job at a travel

---

5. The information in this section is from ITEEN Annual Reports between 2013 and 2016.

agency, I felt I was not making any progress in my life. I fell back spiritually and physically too. My life became a pitiful life.

Then I started off with an ITEEN course. I have felt a lot of change in my life after starting this course. I was able to understand the word of God in an easy way and also to apply it in my life. I understood that God has a plan for my life. Presently, I am studying ITEEN courses next to my job. I have learned to become a trustworthy person, and my boss trusts me more now than he does other colleagues. I am also responsible for a house fellowship, and I am the treasurer of my church.

Tek Ghimire from Kathmandu has also experienced how ITEEN courses have transformed his life.

I am forty years old, and I have a desire to study and learn more from the Bible. I really thank my pastor and leaders for encouraging me to do Bible study. Because of that, I was able to complete three courses of ITEEN: Abundant Life, Abundant Light and The Life of Christ Book One. During my study, I learned about the promises of God given to us and about Jesus and his ministry when he was on earth. The courses of ITEEN help us to do deep Bible study from Genesis to Revelation. It gave us a spiritual and historical knowledge in a way that makes us understand each and every part of the Bible. This helped us to be able to teach and share with others what we learned, and it really encouraged me in my life and ministry and social work.

ITEEN courses are not only working on an individual level in Nepal. One believer understanding the truth of God for his or her life impacts others in the church. Suman Rai says,

I used to think that just because I was born in a Christian family, I was a child of God. But during my study, I came to know that to be a child of God, we have to believe in him and accept him personally in our life. The ITEEN courses opened my eyes. So I repented and accepted Jesus in my life as my Savior. Now I am in the eastern part of Nepal and ministering in the church through teaching ITEEN courses to local church believers.

Suman's story is just one example, but pastors see how believers change when they study ITEEN courses. The Glorious Church of Dhading started running ITEEN courses in 2010. The senior pastor in the church acknowledges that

> It is impossible for believers to grow in faith only through the preaching on Saturday service. They also need some ways of education to grow spiritually as believers. Before the ITEEN courses started in our church, I had to do all the work of the church, and sometimes I even felt hopeless. But through the courses good changes have occurred. Everyone has started taking responsibilities. I can witness to stronger believers who have courage in evangelism. People are more helpful to each other and willing to give of their time and money. The choir group is revived and improved, and people are also able to lead services, so I don't have all the weight on my shoulders.

Going Forward

ITEEN asks you to pray for the protection of the church in Nepal, because right now the law is making it very difficult for them, and they are quite concerned about it. Christians are raising their voices in the United Nations and many other countries asking that they put pressure on Nepal to change the laws. Pray that the church may continue to grow. As it is, there are over 1.5 million Christians in Nepal, and that number is growing day by day. But ITEEN leaders are not serving even one percent of Christians, and they want to serve more people.

Pray and Connect

Please pray

- for protection from the government for the church;
- for fast growth in the number of people that can be served and can serve others;
- for God to continue to guide and use ITEEN.

Institute for Theological Education by Extension in Nepal
Contact address: ITEEN, GPO Box 8975 EPC647, Kathmandu, Nepal
General enquiries: iteen.nepal@gmail.com
Website: http://www.tankasubedi.com.np/Contact

BINAYA'S STORY

with Penelope Vinden

When I was about eleven years old, I went to church for the first time. When I started reading the Bible, I read a verse in Matthew that said you don't have to worry, your Father in heaven will take care of all things. My own father was not with our family. But I always wanted someone who could take care of my needs. So when I read that verse, I thought, "Oh! My grandfather or great-grandfather will hear me!"

© ML Low

When I was old enough for my first TEE course, Abundant Life, it was very useful and simple to understand. Soon I knew who the "Father" is! And when I understood this, I believed in Jesus Christ as my Lord.

After a few years, I read, "Do not worry, you can ask anything, and I will give it to you. But first you need to seek the kingdom of God." I used to ask my heavenly Father for everything, even small things. And there were many blessings. There were problems also – we always get those, and we always need to ask God for help.

There was an incident at the beginning of my high school. The senior girls told me, "You won't do well; you won't be able to get an 80 percent grade. We didn't get it either." I wasn't happy about this and said to myself, "Ok, then I will get 80 percent."

So when the exam came I prayed, "God, I've always been seeking you. I'm always reading the Bible. You've said if we seek the kingdom of God first, we will get everything. So I am praying for a good grade."

When the results came, I got 79.9 percent. I only needed 0.1 percent! My friends said, "Let's check the exam paper." I prayed and said, "God, you can give it to me." So we checked, and a teacher had failed to give me one mark. At that moment I really felt so happy.

You can say that 0.1 percent is a very small thing. But that small thing gave a lot of blessing. I shared my testimony with my friends. I also wrote an essay about this experience and read it in front of my school so I could share the good news of Jesus.

Whenever I'm sad, I always remember that moment. If my heavenly Father can give me that very small thing, he can give me anything.

VIETNAM

17

Vietnam
God Can Work in
Any Circumstance

Graham Aylett and Hanna-Ruth van Wingerden

Background[1]

Vietnam is a communist country in Southeast Asia with over ninety-four million inhabitants. The largest people group by far are the ethnic Vietnamese, who have generally always lived in the lowlands of the country. The highlands are home to many smaller ethnic groups with different cultures to the Vietnamese. One of these groups is the Hmong, which you can read about in chapter 13.

Influences of Confucianism, Daoism, and Buddhism have blended together with indigenous religions in Vietnam. This "Vietnamized Buddhism" with ancestor worship is practiced by over half of the population. In the sixteenth century, Roman Catholic missionaries entered Vietnam, while Protestantism was only introduced in 1911. About 6 percent of the people are Catholic Christians, and around 2 percent are Protestant.

Vietnam has always known some distinction between the South, where Ho Chi Minh City is the largest city, and the North, where Hanoi is the capital.

---

1. The facts in this section are from "Vietnam," Encyclopaedia Britannica, https://www.britannica.com/place/Vietnam, accessed August 2018.

The French colonizers also divided the country into northern and southern parts, but it was in 1954 that the country officially divided into North Vietnam and South Vietnam after a turbulent war of independence from France. The North and South ended up in deep conflict in which the United States was very much involved. The war left Vietnam completely shattered, with a total death toll estimated by some as high as 3.8 million. In 1975 the North won, resulting in communist rule. All foreign missionaries were expelled, and the land became completely closed to Western influence. A difficult time for many Vietnamese people began, and all the more so for believers. Despite all this turmoil, churches continued to grow.

When the Soviet Union collapsed in 1991, the communist government lost its allies. Vietnam's version of perestroika reduced controls on the economy bringing greater economic growth and stability. Gradually the country is becoming more open to influences from abroad, and people in Vietnam are responsive to the gospel. At the same time old cultural practices are resurfacing, and people are also becoming more materialistic as they encounter a capitalistic lifestyle. The government remains watchful and at times hostile to Christians, especially among the minorities.

TEE for the Church in Vietnam

The church has had a very difficult time under the rule of the communist party in Vietnam. Pastors have been persecuted and many detained in re-education camps. In many communities, the communists went to every house and took away every Bible and any Christian literature they could find. It has been impossible for most ethnic minority churches to meet. Thanks to the Lord, the situation has greatly improved, and since 1990 new house churches have come into being.

TEE in Vietnam began in 1992 when Pastor Tran[2] encountered the materials of TEE through Nguyen Anh Tài, President of the Alliance Evangelical Divinity School in California, who visited Vietnam after a request for help to minister in the highlands. Dr Tài brought the six course books of SEAN's The Life of Christ. Tran felt so blessed because this kind of training was exactly the sort of thing

---

2. His name has been changed for security reasons.

that would work in the local circumstances. People can follow the courses in small groups, and they can learn without pastors. It was a safe way for people to learn from the Bible and exactly what was needed. This provision has shown Tran that no problem is too big for God. He can work in each circumstance, no matter how difficult it looks to us. Tran has a large, pastoral heart, and he also has freedom to travel among the different minority groups. From 1992 onwards, Tran has been coordinating a TEE program that has spread widely in Vietnam, largely among the main officially recognized denomination but also among some other groups. This program has now reached over twenty thousand students.

Currently there are twelve TEE coordinating centers connected with the TEE program that Tran coordinates. Each center serves up to a number of provinces and has its own committee. At the moment there are over ten thousand students with around two thousand five hundred studying in the Hmong language, around five hundred in the Dao language, and over seven thousand in Vietnamese TEE courses. The growth of the program is all the more amazing as until 2008, it was illegal to print the TEE courses. One pastor who led groups at that time said,

> I memorized the first three books of The Life of Christ. This was useful when I was with families in persecuted places. We could sit on the floor and be having our discussion without any books. Then if the government police came – it looked as though we were just sitting on the floor for tea and chat. But really it was a TEE group meeting![3]

Since 1992, this TEE program has trained more than a thousand new pastors! Here is what one of them said,

> Over the last fourteen years in my home church, we have run four classes. All the deacons have been through The Life of Christ. We have started these courses in several places in the Mekong delta, and many deacons say, "Thanks to the courses, we have a strong

---

3. Comments in this section were shared at an Increase/SEAN International Vietnamese TEE Consultation, 2018.

foundation." Most of those who have completed The Life of Christ are actively involved in church work and are connected well with other believers.

The Life of Christ series has been used for training in another denomination in Vietnam. Students come together and complete the first three books residentially. Then they are asked to go and share the gospel. They need to provide evidence of at least three or four new believers. But many come back with reports of more, thirty, forty, or even fifty or more. Then they can return and continue studying books four to six. The leader of this denomination estimates that perhaps half a million people have heard the gospel through those who have studied The Life of Christ. Thousands have responded. This leader commented, "When people study The Life of Christ, there are more believers, more churches."

Growth in the Midst of Challenges

Although the program coordinated by Pastor Tran is used in many places in Vietnam, not everyone knows about TEE resources. One example was Pham. Pham is Vietnamese, but he first encountered TEE in Korea. He told us that in general, many churches in Vietnam are young and don't have good discipleship programs. Few people can go to a Bible college and get training. For most, even if they want to learn to study God's word and grow in the knowledge of God, there is no opportunity. Some are not qualified for higher education or can't afford Bible school. That's why TEE is a very suitable program, especially for lay people in rural areas where most of the church planters and church leaders are not well educated. When Pham and a Korean missionary contacted Increase to learn more about the possibilities for TEE in Vietnam, they were invited to Malaysia for some training. Pham said, "I learned so much about TEE and the methodology that makes it so easy to share and reproduce. When we returned to Vietnam, we began using the courses and helping others to be involved."

Pham went on to share some of the things that he sees as important for the development of TEE in Vietnam. First, a wealth of TEE training materials are available across Asia, and some of these may be very useful for Vietnamese believers. A second thing to emphasize is a good knowledge of the methodology that makes TEE so powerful. Group leaders need good skills in facilitating discussion and giving space for their group members to share. Third, it's important to understand that practical application leads to life transformation, and group leaders need to lead the way in putting learning into living.

Pham is encouraged by what he sees the Lord doing through TEE:

> I was leading a group of five students going through Abundant Light. One man told me, "Before I didn't really like reading the Bible. But now, just after a few weeks, I find it so exciting, and I love reading it!" Then also there was a young woman who could only come one time to the course because of a conflict with our meeting and her study schedule. Recently she sent me a message: "Please can you change the schedule. I just came one time, but I was so impressed by the lesson and what we shared. I really want the opportunity to learn!" We couldn't change the time, so now she is looking for friends to start a new group.

Going Forward

In April 2018, Increase worked with a Vietnam network to bring together leaders who are involved with TEE in Vietnam to share their experiences with TEE and their vision for the future. These leaders worked together to agree on a common vision for TEE in Vietnam: *To equip each believer to follow Jesus's example in order to serve communities and develop the church.*

The group chose a TEE Steering Committee of seven people to carry forward TEE work in Vietnam. This committee opens up a wonderful opportunity for different denominations and house church leaders to work together to make TEE resources and relevant TEE training more widely available. The Steering Committee wants to translate some other needed materials into Vietnamese. The Life of Christ is for leadership training, but other TEE courses are relevant and helpful for all church members.

The story of one pastor from the highlands will illustrate the need for grass-roots training. When asked how large his village was, the pastor replied that there were around a thousand people. When asked how many people were in the church he pastors, he replied, "Around a thousand people." This pastor was from a Christian village where the whole community had decided to follow Jesus. TEE materials have already been helping these pastors in their ministry, and praise God for that. But there are other good TEE tools to equip and empower all church members.

Pray and Connect

Please pray
- for the fulfillment of the common vision;
- for the TEE Steering Committee;
- for appropriate new courses and training;
- for TEE groups and group leaders all over Vietnam.

General enquiries: increaseassociation@gmail.com

TEE leaders in a discussion at a conference
© ML Low. Used with permission.

INDONESIA

18

Indonesia
Shine Your Light

Hanna-Ruth van Wingerden

Background[1]

The Indonesian islands are a truly unique area of the world. Situated above a connection between tectonic plates, the country is shaped by volcanoes. The islands serve as a bridge between Asia and Oceania, connecting people from both regions. An incredibly varied environment and society were shaped over time. The national motto, *Bhinneka tunggal ika* (unity in diversity), reflects this variety perfectly, while a shared language and one central government give the idea of unity. Over three hundred different ethnic groups find their home in Indonesia, and most of the world religions, as well as a broad scope of indigenous religions, have followers here.

Indonesia was a Dutch colony and known as the Netherlands East Indies. The country declared its independence in 1945, but it was only in 1949 after a long struggle that the Dutch officially recognized Indonesian autonomy.

Almost nine out of ten people in Indonesia are Muslim. Islam was introduced by traders from the Middle East in the fourteenth century. There are, however, small areas spread out over the country where Christians are

---

1. The facts in this section are from "Indonesia," Encyclopaedia Britannica, https://www.britannica.com/place/Indonesia, accessed August 2018.

dominant. Christianity came to Indonesia through the Dutch and other Europeans. Also, many Chinese people in the cities are Christians. There are often tensions between Christians and Muslims, leading to attacks and violence. Hinduism is the largest religion on the islands of Bali and Lombok. In remote areas, local religions are still widely observed, and for many people, each introduced religion just became an extra layer upon ancient local beliefs.

TEE in Indonesia

It can be a real struggle for the churches to be visible as disciples of Jesus in a Muslim environment. And because Christians are often scattered over the countryside, there can be a lack of unity. Not all churches can afford to pay trained preachers and pastors. If a church has a pastor, the pastor is not always theologically trained. Lack of vision and underdeveloped diaconal ministry can also be real problems for churches, as well as dealing with traditional customs.[2]

TEE in Indonesia was first introduced in the 1970s as part of the first wave of TEE programs spreading across Asia. TEE programs to train church leaders prospered during the late 1970s and 1980s, but then gradually fell into disuse. By 2005, TEE in Indonesia was just a memory for most people, and course books like The Life of Christ were only found on the shelves of libraries.

But since 2006, TEE Korea, with the help of missionaries, has revived TEE ministry in Indonesia. Abundant Life was translated, and a team of facilitators were sent from Korea to lead seminars in a Bible college in Sumatra. Some of the participants liked what they experienced, and they decided to start using foundation level TEE courses. Since then, efforts have been made to use TEE materials for theological education in Bible colleges and churches as TEE Korea continues to work with Indonesian leaders to form Community Learning TEE Indonesia (CLTEE). Taeho Kim, a missionary living in Indonesia, plays an important role in the process.

---

2. "Indonesia," GZB projects, https://www.gzb.nl/projecten-werkvelden, accessed August 2018.

Witnessing in a Muslim Context

Rev Dr Heru Purwanta lives in Boyolali, a small Muslim town about forty kilometres from the capital, Jakarta. His family is the only Christian family in this town of seventy families, and they get on very well with everybody. He said,

> In the town where I live, I was once elected as the leader of my Muslim community for a six-year term. During my tenure, I did my best to be a good leader. Even now, I get on very well with people. Every Christmas, my neighbors help me to cook and serve my guests. And when it is time to celebrate Hari Raya (marking the end of the fasting month for Muslims), I will visit the homes of my Muslim friends. It is really nice to celebrate each other's festivals. Every opportunity for me to gather with my Muslim friends, including going to Quran reading events, are opportunities for me to shine for Christ.[3]

Heru's denomination, Gereja Kristen Jawa Tengah Utara (GKJTU), or Christian Church of Northern Central Java, is one of the churches that has embraced TEE. Today he is the chairman of the GJKTU, which has sixty-two churches and about nine thousand believers. TEE was first introduced in 2015. Initially, a group of twelve leaders met monthly and were trained to be facilitators. Heru said,

> We invited the group of the first twelve leaders for training using Abundant Life and encouraged them all to start a TEE group in their own congregation. After a year, three of them started to roll out TEE programs in their congregations. Interested participants of the first class of Abundant Life will be trained to be facilitators so that they too can start new TEE groups.[4]

---

3. Rev Dr Heru Purwanta interviewed by ML Low at the Increase conference "Empowering Churches, Equipping Disciples," Chiang Mai, 13–17 November 2017.

4. Rev Dr Heru Purwanta said this in a joint interview with Paini, interview by ML Low at the Increase conference "Empowering Churches, Equipping Disciples," Chiang Mai, 13–17 November 2017.

Applying Jesus's Teaching

Rev Dr Heru Purwanta said the following about application:

> We see TEE as an effective method of discipleship. TEE not only teaches but also transforms the participants and in turn leads to growth. When individual lives are transformed, the congregation is also transformed. In a conventional Bible study, usually one person will lead, while only two or three will ask questions, and the majority will just listen. However in TEE, all members participate and do practical homework.
>
> They do not just gain head knowledge but experience faith in action when they apply Jesus's teachings. They also learn that life is not just about being a good Christian who prays and reads the Bible but leaves no impact on others. They become aware that a Christian life is a life of influence, and there is the need to share the good news with others. As TEE is a good program for discipleship, we are excited to roll out our plans to start TEE groups in our congregations. We have all the TEE materials ready in the Indonesian language.[5]

Rev Paini, General Secretary of the GKJTU, also loves the TEE program because she sees how it meets the needs of every Christian and encourages everyone to live a life that affects others. She said,

> What I learned from the program is very practical. For example, when I was in the midst of building my house, a friend approached me for help. She knew of a nineteen-year-old boy (from Sumatra) who was about to be expelled from his dormitory for bad behavior. It was not the best timing for me. But as I reflected on what Jesus would do, I was reminded of the importance of loving others like ourselves. I discussed the matter with my husband and my seventeen-year-old son. Together, we decided to open our home to the boy.[6]

---

5. Heru interview 2017.

6. Rev Paini interview by ML Low at the Increase conference "Empowering Churches, Equipping Disciples," Chiang Mai, 13–17 November 2017.

When Paini subsequently met this boy's teacher, she was told that he had changed for the better. He no longer sleeps in class but is now very attentive. "Jesus's teaching may be very simple, but it has great power to impact lives when we apply them. Through TEE programs, I believe many people will be taught and encouraged, and they will certainly influence the people placed around them."[7]

Pray and Connect

Please pray

- for the GKJTU and other churches that are using TEE materials in Indonesia;
- that they would use them well and see good fruit;
- for good structures and organization to support the TEE work across denominations and for the expansion of the work in more seminaries;
- for translation of new courses.

Community Learning TEE Indonesia
General enquiries:
Reverend Heru: gra_cia19@yahoo.com / +62–813–2920–4562
Reverend Paini: painipeni@yahoo.co.id / +62–857–4168–6493
Missionary Taeho Kim: theo88@daum.net / +62–813–2188–3780

---

7. Paini interview.

PAKISTAN

19

Pakistan
Thriving under Pressure

Tim Green

Background[1]

Pakistan is a land of geographical contrasts – vast mountains, warm and cold deserts, and fertile plains. It is more uniform in regard to religion, however. Officially known as the Islamic Republic of Pakistan, its estimated population of 207 million is more than 96 percent Muslim. So Pakistan has more Muslims than any other nation except Indonesia. Millions live in the megacities of Lahore and Karachi. There are over one hundred people groups and seventy-seven spoken languages, most of which have no written form.

The small Christian minority are not converts but believers who have survived discrimination for generations and now also face religious pressure which breaks out into active persecution at times. Harsh blasphemy laws have been used by extremists to justify violence, whether against fellow Muslims or people of other faiths.

In 2018, because of its severe persecution of Christians, Pakistan was ranked number five on the Open Doors World Watch List. In 2013, two suicide

---

1. The information in this section is from "Pakistan," World Factbook, CIA, https://www.cia.gov/library/publications/the-world-factbook/geos/pk.html, accessed August 2018; and "Pakistan," Country Lists, Operation World, http://www.operationworld.org/country/paki/owtext.html, accessed August 2018.

bombers attacked All Saints Church in Peshawar. Over one hundred and twenty were killed, and more than two hundred and fifty injured. The area coordinator for TEE was one of those who lost his life. The church bombings continue, as do threats, harassment, and violence against families and individuals known to be Christian.

TEE in Pakistan: Open Theological Seminary

In the midst of the many pressures Pakistani Christians face, the national TEE program shines as a beacon of hope. Called the Open Theological Seminary (OTS), it helps believers to not only survive spiritually but to thrive. Every week across the country, hundreds of local TEE groups gather to learn together under the guidance of more than four hundred trained leaders. The learners are from many denominations and every walk of life, and 56 percent are women. "OTS is glad that in a male-dominated society we provide opportunity for women to develop," says OTS Director Dr Qaiser Julius.

In a country where many people are poor and have little or no education, TEE is crucial for creating strong disciples of Christ. Rev Javaid Ilyas, the OTS Course Development Manager, explains:

> TEE is an easy way of doing Bible courses that transform lives. You don't need to leave your house, your job, or your family to get a systematic Bible study program. This is the best way to survive in our country and in the world. Otherwise, if your faith is very shaky and you have little Bible knowledge, I feel it's very tough for you to survive in this world.[2]

TEE also helps Pakistan's Christian minority to have a witness among the majority population. A young woman explains, "Living in this context, people ask us many questions about our faith and beliefs. These courses help me to respond to their questions and express my faith. It's very helpful." A TEE leader confirms that, "If people are equipped, they can be a living testimony among non-Christians. If we have a personal experience of Christ, then wherever we work, whatever we do, Christ will shine from us."

---

2. Javaid Ilyas interview by Denele Ivins, Course Writers Training workshop, June 2018.

OTS was one of the first TEE programs to be established in Asia, starting in 1971. It offers a connected learning pathway of courses to help new believers grow gradually into godly leaders. Since its inception, around thirty thousand Pakistani Christians have completed at least one OTS course, including three thousand students in the teenagers' program. Currently there are six thousand active students, and the number grows each year.

Deir Mar Thoma Institute

Another member of the Increase Association in Pakistan is Deir Mar Thoma: The Open School of Missional Formation. Founded by Zafar Ismail, a former Director of OTS, its vision is "Mentoring disciples of Christ in a Muslim context for living out a missional lifestyle in a witnessing community in the power of the Spirit; imitating Christ in the daily walk, engaging in a constructive dialogue, proclaiming Christ and making disciples, and responding to human needs by loving service." Deir Mar Thoma is currently developing a missional curriculum for an Islamic context.

TEE in the Service of the Church

In the past the greatest challenge for OTS was acceptance by churches. Pastors saw TEE as a threat or rival to their own authority. However after many years of hard work, churches now appreciate the work of OTS. As students progress through the curriculum, they are equipped to serve their churches actively. A pastor in a frontier province testifies, "I can see a big difference in the lives of my church families. They are now more involved in church activities, leaving their shyness behind. I have also observed that many of the families of my church are demonstrating positive change in their daily lives. These are the families of those students who have studied OTS courses."

A remarkably wide range of denominations use OTS courses, and this has helped to reduce the barriers between them. One pastor who has served for twenty-five years remarks, "Before doing this course, I was thinking that my denomination was the best. The rest were not as spiritual. But now I have respect for other churches as well – we are all part of the body of Christ. Now I'm willing to have fellowship with other churches."

Transformation through TEE[3]

In Pakistan to be "Christian" often means just to belong to the Christian community, in contrast to being Muslim. TEE courses challenge all Christians to commit whole-heartedly to following Jesus and be distinctive in their lifestyle rather than Christians in name only.

Rev Nadeem Masih heads up the OTS field department. Last year he met a Christian policeman whose behavior had been changed through studying the course Abundant Life. This man shared his testimony: "When I began to take this course, I realized that actually I am a corrupt man. . . . After taking this course, I committed myself to the Lord. Now I will be faithful in my work and also in what I earn. I will not take bribes anymore."

On his travels, Nadeem also met a Christian lawyer who said, "Many people come to me for a divorce. I insist that first we have a counselling session. I encourage them to talk with me at no cost, and I advise them not to pursue divorce. Many of the couples stop pursuing the divorce, and so families are not broken." This man, who is not from a wealthy family, gives his time and energy and doesn't care about his fee. He has a passion to help his community because of the courses he has taken.

OTS as an Example for TEE in Asia

The Open Theological Seminary is notable for three reasons.

1. Writing Many New Courses

Over a forty-year period, OTS has written nearly thirty courses of its own and has contextualized another twenty. To write a completely new course from nothing is a challenging task indeed and takes a long time. But progress speeded up after OTS formed its own course development department in 2000. They deal with local topics, such as the course on folk religion. Church history is taught not from a Western angle but from Asian and Pakistani perspectives and relates the lessons to today's issues. Currently the team is writing a new course on Christian responses to persecution and suffering.

---

3. The material and quotes in this section were shared by Rev Nadeem Masih at the Increase conference "Empowering Churches, Equipping Disciples," Chiang Mai, 13–17 November 2017.

OTS broke new ground in contextual course writing when it launched a whole ten-course curriculum for Pakistani Christian youth that was created by first researching their concerns and then written directly in Urdu. As the OTS Director, Qaiser Julius, explains, "It is a very contextualized program. Our younger generation need to understand their identity in Christ, that they are part of that Pakistani soil. The program is holistic, with courses relating to the spiritual and the environmental, to society and identity. It is going very well."[4]

OTS has gained expertise in course writing and is happy to share it with others. Two of its courses were given to SEAN who published them as Abundant Light and Feed My Lambs. These courses have brought worldwide blessing in many languages. More recently OTS's experience, through its staff member Freda Carey as an Increase Equipper, has contributed to Increase's program to train a new generation of TEE course writers in Asia (see chapter 30).

2. Creating a Connected Learning Pathway

OTS has certificate, diploma, and bachelor of theology programs of TEE courses, all accredited by the Asia Theological Association. Importantly, these levels link up one to the next. Those who start with the basic courses gain confidence to continue on to the higher ones. Progressively the learning becomes more challenging as students are equipped to compare and evaluate sources, think for themselves, write more difficult assignments, and finally carry out an original research project.

This provision of a joined-up learning pathway has had remarkable results. For example, Rashid came from a poor, nominally Christian family and never went to school. But later after coming to a living faith, he longed to be able to read the Bible for himself. Someone taught him to read and write, and at the age of twenty-two, he started his first TEE course. You can read more about him in chapter 32.

Today Pastor Rashid serves Christian background brick factory workers who live on the outskirts of Lahore. They have a very low status and are very poor. But some have joined TEE groups under Pastor Rashid's leadership. One brick maker's son has now studied ten TEE courses and is helping to encourage

---

4. Shared by Qaiser Julius at the Increase conference, "Empowering Churches, Equipping Disciples," Chiang Mai, 13–17 November 2017.

and teach Christians in three factories. Three men became pastors in a village area in the countryside with the Brethren Church. Three more are ministers with Pastor Rashid, and his own daughter teaches in Sunday school.

At the beginning, Rashid was not qualified to enter a traditional seminary. But the Open Theological Seminary's connected pathway of leadership training allowed him to grow academically, flourish in his gifts, and in turn help others flourish. While opening a pathway to the higher academic levels, OTS has not ignored learners at the other end. Many Pakistani Christians in rural areas can't read or write, so taking a TEE course seems impossible. As head of the field department, Nadeem Masih feels they couldn't neglect this large group of people:

> So we are making a plan to bring TEE to them. We explored some storytelling methods, but often the questions are too simple and can just be answered with one or two words. We want to include the discussion and practical components that are crucial to the TEE methodology. We will train the group leaders to do everything orally, but there are many challenges! A few of them have smart phones, so we are exploring different technologies.[5]

3. Partnership with Theological Institutions

OTS has positive relationships with several seminaries and Bible colleges in Pakistan and has played a key role in a network of theological educators. An example is Zarephath Bible Seminary which intentionally included OTS courses as part of their three-year training of pastors. Their former principal Rev Ashkenaz Asif Khan explains why they did this:

> There were several reasons: the courses are well-structured, and the students learn a new method of learning as well as teaching. The Open Theological Seminary TEE is widespread over the country; thus our students must be aware of this new market. Our students are qualified to teach TEE as soon as they leave

---

5. Nadeem Masih interview by Penny Vinden at the Increase conference "Empowering Churches, Equipping Disciples," Chiang Mai, 13–17 November 2017.

the seminary. This makes them better equipped for ministry in the city or town. We are doing what is best for our students and what helps the kingdom cause. The graduates become cutting-edge workers all over the country offering viable teaching tools. This is a win-win partnership for the glory of our Master, Jesus Christ.[6]

In addition to these three examples, there are other ways in which OTS's half century of experience can benefit newer TEE movements. It has pioneered ways to assess student growth in character and skills, not just knowledge. It trains TEE group leaders not through a one-time event but through a progressive series of trainings, while also encouraging them through local visits and public recognition. And the OTS system of area coordinators enables it to extend the work to even far-flung regions that are remote from its central office. OTS makes a significant contribution to TEE in Asia through the Increase Association. OTS Director Qaiser Julius is a member of the Increase Committee and an Increase Equipper. He also speaks on behalf of Increase in the Asia Theological Association.

Pray and Connect

Please pray
- for the leadership team to have energy and wisdom to take the work forward;
- that Pakistani Christians equipped through OTS and Deir Mar Thoma may be joyful witnesses in this overwhelmingly Muslim nation.

Open Theological Seminary
General enquiries: openseminary@gmail.com
Website: http://www.ots-trust.org

Deir Mar Thoma
General enquiries: deir.mar.thoma@btinternet.com

---

6. Rev Ashkenaz Asif Khan, email to Graham Aylett, 21 March 2014.

RAHILA'S STORY

with Penelope Vinden

Rahila has been working for ten years with the Open Theological Seminary (OTS) in Pakistan. She works in records – checking exams, making certificates, and putting data on the computer for more than six thousand students. She makes it sound like just a clerical job, but then she adds, almost shyly, "I also teach some courses. Oh yes, and I do group leader training. I just want to serve my God."

"I come from a small village. The people there have many needs – they are not educated, and their financial situation is not good. The children want to get education, but they have no choice; there is only a small primary school. Many women work for Muslim families but don't earn enough to pay school fees. I would like to do something for the women, perhaps sewing classes so they can get a steady income. I would like to do something to help. I don't know what yet, but I pray to God – please guide and help me, please show me what to do."

"Since my childhood I have had a vision to do something for God. I feel happy in my heart doing this – that I am not just earning money, but serving God."

"Sometimes difficulties come in life. Then I sit alone and speak to God, and I realize – don't worry, because you are working for God. We see in the Bible that God says, 'If you are my followers you will face many problems, but don't worry. I am with you, and I will show you the path.' So I feel joy knowing that God is with me."

"I love the story of God calling Moses. God says he is sending him to save his people, and Moses says, 'No, no, no. I can't speak. I have no ideas.' He has all kinds of excuses. But God says, 'No – you go because I am with you. I become your mouth. I give you words.' These things give me strength and encourage me. This is how I face troubles in my life and never let them distract me from my passion for serving God."

Building Stronger Churches

Healthy churches require well-trained, godly leaders: not just one pastor per church, but a group of leaders with complementary ministries. Often these are lay people who develop into ministry while continuing in their jobs. TEE is well suited to help. This section describes five TEE movements which use varying approaches and curricula to help churches equip local leaders in their own contexts. Actually, most of the countries listed in other sections also equip leaders, countries like Thailand, Bangladesh, Pakistan, Vietnam, and China.

PHILIPPINES

20

Philippines
Inspiring and
Supporting Believers

Graham Aylett and Hanna-Ruth van Wingerden

Background

The Philippines were named after Philip II, the king of Spain at the time of the Spanish colonization of the island group. Having been under Spanish rule for centuries, and under US guidance for almost fifty years, the Philippines have many cultural ties with the West. English is an official language, and it is one of only two predominantly Roman Catholic countries in Asia. However, Filipinos are Asian in the way they look at life and are ethnically very diverse. No one is sure how many different native languages and dialects are spoken in the Philippines, but studies suggest that there are at least one hundred and fifty. Tagalog is the most commonly spoken language.[1]

Contemporary Filipinos live in an economic contradiction: the country has incredible riches, but these are not divided well. Some people live in extreme wealth while many live in devastating poverty. Poverty feeds other problems

---

1. "Philippines," Encyclopaedia Britannica, https://www.britannica.com/place/Philippines, accessed August 2018.

like drug-related crimes and violence. The sex industry, apparently the fourth largest source of income, keeps many people captive.[2]

Challenges for the Church

Over 90 percent of Filipinos are Roman Catholic, and about 10 percent belong to other Christian denominations. A major challenge for evangelical churches – mostly first-generation churches – is spiritual maturity. First-generation church leaders have maturity in some areas, for example church planting, but need the support and experience of others in other areas like staying true to biblical teaching and practices when local custom and tradition are animist. There is a danger of "slipping back" into old traditions.

TEE Programs Serving the Church[3]

One of the longest standing programs is the Christian and Missionary Alliance Churches of the Philippines (CAMACOP). CAMACOP runs the Alliance Theological Education by Extension program which was designed to train pastoral leaders and held its first classes in 1976. Rev Edward Cruz, the Head of Non-residential Pastoral Training, reports that there are over three hundred centers and around two thousand students currently in the program. The Head of the Educational Division of CAMACOP, Dr Averell Aragon, says, "We are really focused. We use TEE for training in evangelism, church planting, and mission. My vision is that everyone who graduates from Bible college will have had an experience of TEE and be able to use it in their ministry."

The President of CAMACOP, Bishop Eduardo Cajes, was one of the Alliance TEE staff in the 1990s who travelled by motorbike to visit the TEE centers, deliver course materials, and encourage the leaders. "TEE is my passion!" he says. As President of CAMACOP, he wants to encourage the denomination to use the materials that he has seen build up so many leaders.

---

2. "Philippines," Operation World, http://www.operationworld.org/country/phil/owtext.html, accessed August 2018.

3. This section is based on a meeting with CAMACOP leaders in Metro Manila, Philippines, February 2018.

Another smaller TEE group is the Bethany Fellowship in Cauayan. Bethany has been using TEE for around thirty years. They use Ilokano translations of the basic, practical, and foundational training and have begun to share their experience with churches of some other denominations. Bethany Fellowship has been encouraged by just how open and active in ministry those who finish TEE courses are and realized that other churches could benefit from this training. "All our active members – those who are willing to be part of the ministry – studied Abundant Life and Abundant Light," explains Rosana Longgat, Director of TEE at the Bethany Fellowship. "We don't need to push or encourage them towards ministry – the courses themselves generate their desire to work in ministry."[4]

Rosana Longgat is also an Increase Equipper and helped with training in Vietnam. Increase has helped bring together different users of TEE in the Philippines.

Transformed Lives and Congregations

Pastor Nanding is a church leader who attended a TEE group leader training session run by Bethany Fellowship. He shared how he felt after the training and was very emotional when he spoke:

> It has had a big impact on me as a facilitator because I already teach Abundant Life in my church. But this is so good. God has given me a vision from the book of Colossians 1:28. He touched my heart, and gave me the task to present everyone perfect in Christ! I have a big responsibility. If I have no knowledge of God's word, how can I present the people perfect in Christ? So I praise God for this training. Praise the Lord![5]

Pastor Nanding's wife recently trained as a TEE group leader to help her husband in pioneering in the rural village setting where they serve.

---

4. Rosana Longgat quoted in Joanne Lane, "Sharing TEE in the Philippines," *GO Magazine* (July 2015): 11.
5. Heard by Graham Aylett at a training at Bethany Fellowship in January 2015.

Another pastor from the capital city, Manila, launched the courses in his church. Pastor Jonathan says,

> In 2015, we started The Life of Christ, and we fell in love with the material. We received reports of how lives were transformed. Early 2018, we started Abundant Life in church. My own daughter came to me and told me that now she understood what Christian faith is. She has been listening to my preaching all her life, but she never truly understood her faith until doing the Abundant Life course.[6]

Although Pastor Jonathan lives in the capital, he is taking The Life of Christ to groups of pastors in the countryside area where he grew up. One of the pastors in his group there, Pastor Elbert, travels in from his home on a remote island where most are fishermen and a few work for the government. After completing Book One of The Life of Christ, Pastor Elbert used some of the things he had been learning in a Sunday sermon. Pastor Elbert said that his members were so surprised by his message. They said, "The pastor did his homework. He studied well for his sermon." On that particular Sunday, there was a visitor from the city. He was so impressed by the new things he learned from the pastor's message that he gave him a love gift of almost one hundred dollars! This was a real encouragement to Pastor Elbert. Pastor Jonathan is so happy to hear how the Lord is using the materials to bring change to the church leaders. The first batch are graduating soon.

Reaching More Churches

Bethany Fellowship and others are working to develop an interdenominational, national TEE network that can connect and provide encouragement for TEE users all across the Philippines, the Institute for Theological Education by Extension, Philippines (ITEEP). The ITEEP team have already translated the Abundant Life and Abundant Light courses into Tagalog, a national language of the Philippines. "The younger generations in the Philippines, especially in our city, prefer to use Tagalog instead of the local language. So although our

---

6. Pastor Jonathan, shared at the Increase conference "Empowering Churches, Equipping Disciples," Chiang Mai, 13–17 November 2017.

elders still prefer to use Ilokano, we feel it is also important to meet the needs of the younger generations," says Rosana Longgat.

The ITEEP team hopes to reach more churches in their area and beyond. Finding funds for this is a challenge, as is convincing church leaders to try their program. But the team is confident that the numbers of students and the witness of those involved will speak for themselves.

CAMACOP have a tremendous vision to see TEE centers established in each and every C&MA church across the Philippines – which would mean around three thousand TEE centers. And in the future, CAMACOP would like to train TEE course writers to enrich their current curriculum with new courses for their context. Let's join TEE users in the Philippines in praying that the Lord would impact business people through TEE and call them to use their experience to help spread the blessings!

Pray and Connect

Please pray
- for the establishment of TEE centers in C&MA churches across the Philippines;
- for new writers to write new contextualized courses;
- for the impact of TEE on people who will be able to help spread it;
- for the fulfillment of CAMACOP's vision for a TEE center in every church;
- for the developing TEE network in the Philippines to fruitfully bring different TEE users together.

Christian and Missionary Alliance Churches of the Philippines
General inquiries: Rev Edward Cruz, National Director, Non Residential Training Institution of CAMACOP, edclagao@yahoo.com

TEE in Bethany Fellowship and Institute for Theological Education by Extension in the Philippines:
General Inquiries: Rosana Longgat, rosana_longgat@yahoo.com, or ring +63–9171472524 or +63–9178814901

PAPUA NEW GUINEA

21

Papua New Guinea Contextualized Training for Church Leaders

Graham Aylett and Hanna-Ruth van Wingerden

Background[1]

Papua New Guinea is one of the most culturally diverse countries in the world. Located in the southwestern Pacific, the country encompasses the eastern half of the island of New Guinea and its offshore islands. Over a period of thousands of years, many different people colonized the islands. Language is but one of the traces they left, and over eight hundred different native languages are spoken. The official languages are English, Tok Pisin (Pidgin language), and Hiri Motu.

Most of the people live across the diverse rural landscape in small villages. The extended family is one of the pillars of life. These families, in many cases, are part of a clan. Unfortunately, inter-clan warfare and feuding continue up until today in the highland provinces, and in those areas these conflicts often shape the political parties and views in modern day elections.

---

1. The facts in this section are from "Papua New Guinea," Encyclopaedia Britannica, https://www.britannica.com/place/Papua-New-Guinea, accessed August 2018; and "Papua New Guinea," Operation World, http://www.operationworld.org/country/papu/owtext.html, accessed August 2018.

Nearly all of Papua New Guinea's people are Christian, at least nominally. More than 40 percent of the population is Protestant, and approximately 20 percent are Roman Catholic. Seventh-day Adventism is increasing in popularity, and the country is a target for Muslim missionaries. Despite the influence of Christianity, many people also maintain traditional religious beliefs. Rituals of magic, spells, and sorcery are still widely practiced.

Challenges for the Church

These traditional beliefs are one of the challenges for the church in Papua New Guinea. Another great challenge is education. It is not compulsory to go to school, and the state does not offer free education. Many people, including pastors, never received a full education. The many small and scattered villages also make it difficult to build a church where people experience a sense of unity with fellow believers, and harder for pastors to serve their scattered congregations. One church leader in Papua New Guinea wrote recently,

> I believe Papua New Guinea seems fully evangelized, but this is only true at first glance. What we need in Papua New Guinea churches today is a deeper understanding of God's word. We are reminded of Hosea 4:6 where it states: "My people are destroyed from lack of knowledge" (NIV). Lack of God's knowledge has made many of our church leaders and members of congregations dry. The zeal, enthusiasm, and the drive seemed to have faded. There is a spiritual hunger for sound teachings of God's word across our denominations.[2]

---

2. Isaac Pulupe, "Foreword," in *Christian Leaders' Training College Theological Education by Extension Prospectus*, revised July 2018.

TEE in Papua New Guinea[3]

The Christian Leaders' Training College (CLTC) has used TEE in Papua New Guinea since the 1970s. CLTC is an evangelical, interdenominational Bible and theological college that was founded in 1965. After the first TEE pilot course in English, the number of students, courses, and extension centers was expanded. The TEE program is called Distance Education. CLTC TEE has helped many to develop their gifts and serve more meaningfully. Many TEE students have a closer walk with the Lord Jesus, and hundreds have made personal commitments to follow Jesus Christ. In 2018, over sixteen thousand students completed one or more courses.

Pastors and church leaders taking TEE courses can have a huge impact on the church they are serving. "Who is this fellow preaching? Which Bible college did he attend? He preaches so well!" remarked a curious theology student to a fellow classmate in the middle of the sermon in a local church one Sunday.

The reply was, "He never went to a Bible college, but did TEE courses at home!"

The curious student exclaimed, "Man! None of our classmates could preach like this!"

Ordinary men and women like this pastor are equipped and empowered through their study of TEE courses so that churches are able to flourish.

Making Disciples and Planting Churches[4]

A very clear example of how TEE has helped churches is that of the Evangelical Brotherhood Church (EBC) of Papua New Guinea. EBC has caught the vision of TEE and as a result experienced a period of rapid growth in the 1990s and early 2000s. Ulrich and Christina Spycher tell the story:

---

3. The material in this section is from a case study presented by Philip Bungo, at that time Director of Distance Theological Education by Extension, Papua New Guinea, to the Increase conference, "Twenty-First Century TEE in Asia: Challenges and Opportunities," Kathmandu, October 2010.

4. The material in this section is also from a case study presented by Philip Bungo, Director of Distance Theological Learning at Christian Leaders' Training College of Papua New Guinea, to the Increase conference, "Twenty-First Century TEE in Asia: Challenges and Opportunities," Kathmandu, October 2010.

Our first contact with the TEE program goes back to the 1970s. It looked very promising, and we decided to run a pilot project of a new course in our church. From that first pilot course, we moved on to regular TEE ministry as part of our yearly program with a rapid growth of EBC church work in the area. Our commitment to the program also grew: time has shown that the TEE ministry produced a lasting impact in the lives of many students and young people who attended these courses. TEE is tutored by elders and pastors in their own local congregations and in major prisons around the country.[5]

Through the years of using TEE courses, the impact on people can be clearly seen. *Come Follow Me* is the name of a course written especially for the context in Papua New Guinea. It has brought a large number of students to personal conviction and acceptance of Christ as their personal Savior and friend. This is where spiritual and life transformation takes place. One pastor shares, "I have been a pastor for the last fifteen years, and I never knew who Jesus really was until after I did this course, when I came to know him in a personal way." This pastor's testimony is just one of many similar stories. The fact that people really learn what it means to follow Jesus is so important in a country where Christianity is often a nominal religion and mixed with animist practices from ancient beliefs.

TEE encourages and supports church planting and has enabled many students who do not have theological degrees or diplomas to plant churches in their own areas. Philip Bungo was converted in prison in 1982 after he studied *Come Follow Me*. When he was released from prison with the knowledge he had gained from the TEE studies, he went home and shared his new-found faith in Christ. He had no formal education, but the church grew. In the space of fourteen years, six local churches were planted. He later joined the staff of the CLTC TEE program and served with them for a number of years.

TEE is often the only way that pastors and church leaders can get theological education. Full-time study is not always an option because they live in remote areas and many only ever received a few years of basic education. And how can

---

5. Ulrich Spycher, Christina Spycher, *Singaut Magazine* 157 (Sept–Dec 2007): 1–15.

they study full time while still continuing in their pastoral ministry? The fact that TEE can be done where they are is immensely helpful. Also the simple English style and contextualization helps students to grasp the content, despite their basic level of English. Residential Bible college graduates are often not so keen to minister in remote settings, but TEE courses can help equip people who are already living and serving there.

TEE courses have changed the way that ordinary people think. They discover things in the Bible that other readers don't find, and what's more, they put what they find into practice in daily life. TEE is well known for being practical and not just theoretical. Students can apply the new insights in their own context immediately instead of waiting a long time until after they graduate, which helps them grow as whole-life disciples. Many ordinary TEE students have gained divine wisdom and insight in rightly handling the word of God. They are now able to teach and preach in ways that are recognized and admired. TEE has indeed enabled ordinary people to relate to and live by the Bible.

The need for the kinds of training that CLTC TEE provides is great. In the past many have benefitted from these courses. Today there are three CLTC campuses, all offering TEE, although the main program is in Banz in the highlands. The other campuses are in Port Moresby, the national capital, and in Lae.

Pray and Connect

Please pray

- for all staff involved in TEE work;
- for all those leading and studying TEE courses in Papua New Guinea;
- for believers to be salt and light and not Christians in name only.

Christian Leaders' Training College
General enquiries: Isaac Pulupe, ipulupe@cltc.ac.pg
Website: https://www.cltc.ac.pg/

INDIA

22

India
Training Believers
of All Levels

David Ball and Hanna-Ruth van Wingerden

Background[1]

India is a diverse country where countless numbers of small ethnicities and tribes find their home. Many Indians express their identities mainly through religion. Hinduism is the main religion of modern India, and it can be traced back to the Indo-Aryan people who migrated to the Indus Valley in around 1500 BC and who assimilated the ancient religions and cultures of the Indus Valley civilization that existed from 2600 BC.

Christianity has almost certainly existed in India from the sixth century AD, although Syrian Christians in India even trace their origin to the apostle Thomas, who is said to have brought the gospel to India around AD 50. Overall, about 2.3 percent of India's population is Christian. Much later Islam brought by Arab, Turkish, and Persian invaders beginning in the eighth century became influential. Islam was there to stay, and by the thirteenth century, much of the

---

1. The facts in this section are from "India," Wikipedia, https://en.wikipedia.org/wiki/India, accessed August 2018; "India," Encyclopaedia Britannica, https://www.britannica.com/place/India, accessed August 2018; and "India," Operation World, http://www.operationworld.org/country/indi/owtext.html, accessed August 2018.

country was ruled by Muslims. When India became independent in 1947, the subcontinent was divided into two countries – India with a majority of Hindus and Pakistan with a majority of Muslims. The eastern part of Pakistan later became Bangladesh.

Twenty-two official languages are listed in the Constitution of India, and the 2001 census of India shows that 122 major languages are spoken. In addition are 1,599 languages and dialects.

India is a growing economy; nevertheless, there is much inequality in the division of wealth. The majority of people live in rural areas. However, India has three of the biggest and most diverse cities in the world – Mumbai (Bombay), Kolkata (Calcutta), and Delhi.

The Need for Theological Training

In view of the growing number of new believers and increasing pressure from various ideologies, training Christian workers is an important need that is essential in the long term. The life and health of the church depend on the proper development of pastors, teachers, evangelists, and missionaries. In churches, poor discipling and lack of teaching and modelling of biblical life and leadership are problems.

The house church movement reports phenomenal growth throughout India in terms of the number of new churches, especially among people groups who have been excluded from mainstream society. The leaders of most of these house churches and community churches are themselves new believers. Many of these believers become leaders without a thorough knowledge of the word of God and without the tools necessary to disciple other believers. Training local church leadership for mission and ministry continues to be an urgent priority for the church in India.

TEE in India

TEE is filling this need for training. The Association for Theological Education by Extension (TAFTEE) has been providing discipleship and leadership training to the churches since 1971. Through their courses, many churches have benefitted because their pastors and leaders can complete the courses without leaving home for a residential seminary, and their lay people can be equipped for discipleship in the midst of everyday life.

Apart from TAFTEE, TEE courses are used by other institutions as well. The Union Biblical Seminary (UBS) in Pune offers an MDiv in English and a BTh in Marathi. The Assemblies of God college in Bangalore, the Southern Asia Bible College, also offers a distance learning MDiv as part of the Global School of Distance Learning. In addition, YWAM in India have also started using TEE courses.

TAFTEE today offers training programs in nine different languages to new believers, lay leaders, pastors, cross-cultural missionaries, and grass-roots level Christian workers. There are currently twelve thousand students at different levels throughout India and neighboring countries. The courses range from foundational and certificate level to bachelor, master and postgraduate level. All these courses aim to build up the local church and make it healthier and stronger. A network of over one thousand five hundred volunteer group leaders serve as facilitators for the group discussions that are crucial to TEE. Increase has supported TAFTEE by providing new models for group leader training. Most study sessions are sponsored and hosted by local churches.

Training for Every Believer[2]

The TEE courses are open to any student regardless of their educational background, level of income, gender, denomination, or caste. To make this study available to people from all backgrounds, scholarships are provided to people from lower-income groups. TAFTEE also translates the material into local languages, so people who do not know English can also study the material. While studying, the students learn to understand the teachings of the Christian faith based on the Bible. This knowledge is not just academic; it is embedded in the church so students directly improve their effectiveness in ministry.

An example is the course on house groups. The students are expected to start a house group for at least ten weeks, and some of these groups have evolved into local churches. The courses that are used in India have all been adapted

---

2. The content in this section was shared by David Samuel, Director of TAFTEE, at the Increase conference "Empowering Churches, Equipping Disciples," Chiang Mai, 13–17 November 2017.

to suit the local situation. Although courses like Following Jesus (The Life of Christ) are translated, the examples and illustrations are all contextualized so people understand them immediately. The courses are making the best use of scholarly tools and educational technology to enable students to enhance the effectiveness of their ministry.

Most of the TEE courses in India are developed and designed in the country, particularly at the degree level. And some courses have been translated and adapted for use in countries like Bangladesh, Pakistan, Sri Lanka, Mongolia, and even the UK. The most significantly used course (about nine thousand students at any one time) is Following Jesus (The Life of Christ), and it is available in nine different languages. These same books are used by a number of evangelical Bible schools for their own training courses. TAFTEE has adapted this two-year integrated course for the Indian context using Indian pictures, Indian examples, and Indian stories.

Other courses have also been adapted with culturally appropriate changes so the courses are relevant for the Indian situation. Students who have taken this course have been greatly encouraged and blessed in their lives and ministries. "I have learned things that I have never thought of, and my presentation of the gospel to unreached people has totally changed. I am also sure that my ministry is growing, and I am personally being blessed," says Rohit Singh from Uttaranchal after studying Following Jesus. Saleem, who used to be Muslim but is now a Christian, says, "The Following Jesus course has helped me to differentiate between the teachings of Islam and the Christian interpretation of the Bible."

Training for Church Leaders

TAFTEE is embraced by many denominational churches in India and has been a strong voice for evangelical faith within those churches. Some of them accept TAFTEE as their lay training program, and some accept it for ordination as well. TAFTEE is accredited by the Asia Theological Association for bachelor and master level courses. The bachelor of theological studies (BTS), master of divinity, and master of theology programs are aimed at those who are actively involved in voluntary and full-time ministry at the local church level. Pastor Isaac Samuel, a missionary and church planter from Punjab, says, "TAFTEE enables me to understand the exact meaning of God's word and trains me to teach it appropriately to my congregation."

Malcolm Athishtam is one of TAFTEE's BTS graduates, and he shares:

> I first encountered TEE after completing my degree in engineering. I was looking for a place to study the Bible in depth, and a friend introduced me to the TAFTEE course being conducted in my church. For the past thirty years, I have been associated both as a student and a facilitator. For someone who could have never attended a seminary to study theology, TEE was the best alternative. I have been working at the South Asia Institute of Advanced Christian Studies for the past four years. However, I would still choose TEE over a residential degree if I was to do it all again. Let me explain why. First, theology is not studied in isolation but learned in the market place. With TEE courses, we apply what we learn immediately. Second, TEE does not have one teacher or expert from whom everyone learns, but everyone, including the facilitators, become teachers during the group study. Each participant brings a varied understanding which enriches the learning process. The courses in BTS were so well written and comprehensive that it ensured a sound theological grounding for life to witness in the world. I am so blessed by the ministry of TAFTEE. My life, vision, and impact for God's kingdom has grown manifold, and I continue to be a witness and live for the glory of God.

A BTS and MTh graduate of TAFTEE, Ingrid Solomon testifies,

> Having come from a Roman Catholic background, I required a mature understanding and comprehension of Scripture and evangelism techniques. These I gained considerably during my BTS through TAFTEE. However, for actual ministerial work in my ministry in the secular media of this nation, the TAFTEE M.Th. course is a real blessing. The faculty are excellent, the worth of the group discussions is immeasurable, and I have gained much in

confidence, know-how, and sensitivity regarding how to proceed with my ministry.

Pray and Connect

Please pray

- for the Director and staff of TAFTEE as they coordinate the TEE ministry;
- for regional TAFTEE organizing committees as they serve churches and groups in their areas;
- for the many TAFTEE group leaders and students in different parts of India.

The Association for Theological Education by Extension, India
General enquiries: taftee@taftee.net
Postal address: TAFTEE, #90/1 Robertson Road, Frazertown, Bangalore 560005, India
Phone number: +91–8028465034

A TEE class in Cambodia

CHINA

23

China
Equipping Leaders to
Train More Leaders

Hanna-Ruth van Wingerden

Background[1]

The biggest of all Asian countries with the most extensive population of any country in the world is China. It is a multinational country: the people comprise a variety of ethnic and linguistic groups of which the Han Chinese is the largest. China has been a center of religious ideas and systems: Confucianism and Daoism (Taoism) originated here and influenced Chinese society and government for centuries. Buddhism found its way into China very early on.

From 1949 onwards with the establishment of the People's Republic of China by the Chinese Communist Party, the country closed its doors to the world. Communism affected the influence of these religions, but also affected Christians. At that time, out of an estimated population of four hundred and fifty million, there were only about five hundred thousand baptized Christians in China. The country became officially atheist, although state-monitored religious practices continued to be allowed.

---

1. The information in this section is from "China," Operation Mobilisation, https://www.om.org/en/country-profile/china, accessed August 2018; and "China," Encyclopaedia Britannica, https://www.britannica.com/place/China, accessed August 2018.

Since the late 1970s, China has become more open to the world outside, most of all through the international economy. Today China is one of the great players in the international market. As China opened up more, economic reforms also resulted in mass migrations to the cities. Urban life creates more challenges but also more opportunities for people in their working and spiritual life.

A Growing Church

Today Christians are a small but significant and growing minority in China. Their numbers have increased to well over one hundred million! This fast growth is something to be incredibly thankful for, but at the same time it can lead to a lack of Bible knowledge and false teachings.

The government is also keeping a closer eye on citizens and churches. Religious laws have been passed that make church life very difficult. All the big churches are going to gradually disappear from China as it is getting more and more difficult to rent any premises. No landlord dares to rent to the church, so the big churches are becoming small cell group churches.

Many Chinese believers also live outside of China, and they have their own churches in many European countries and America. Also across Asia, for example in Malaysia and Indonesia, are Chinese communities and churches. Chinese churches want to be a place of worship for Chinese immigrants and their descendants in these countries.

TEE in China: A Tried and Tested Method

TEE Movers for the Chinese Church (TMCC) are working not only with churches in China, but also with Chinese churches in twenty-four other countries. TMCC was created in 1997 when Pastor Shim Hong in California decided to translate the TEE materials into Chinese as one of his church's mission projects. He went on to train Korean missionaries to lead TEE groups in China. In 2006, Chinese-American Pastor Jason and Jane Lee[2] travelled with Pastor and Mrs Shim to China to lead classes and receive on-the-job training.

---

2. Their names have been changed for security reasons.

When Jason was expelled from China in 2012, he and Jane relocated to Taipei where they revised the old translations and made more translations of the new TEE books that opened the materials for Chinese believers in countries outside China. The Lees are constantly on the move. For most of the year they are on the road training group leaders in seminaries, house churches, businessmen's groups, registered churches, denominational churches, and mission organizations.[3]

Jason and Jane focus their attention mainly on church leaders and people with decision-making power, because they can take TEE forward in their own churches. Jason explains,

> We go to a church and introduce TEE to the leaders by using a well-prepared presentation with testimonies. We really try to light a spark through the presentation about The Life of Christ courses. Sometimes we treat them to lunch or dinner after this initial introduction, so we can build up a relationship. Finally, we ask them to try to study one unit. The idea of months of study to finish all the books can be a bit daunting, so we just ask them to try it for one session of ninety minutes. Then after that they decide if it is good for their church.[4]

When the senior pastor or leader has decided to roll out the courses, Jason and Jane come in. They give a very intensive group facilitator training, where they ask three or four churches to send their leaders and decision makers to the session to form groups of twelve to sixteen people. They explain, "Three months before we give the training, we give them the book, and they do all the self-study for one course at home. When we get there, we lead the class in ten units over just three days."

After these sessions, the group facilitators in training do extra homework for each book, for example drawing a map of Jesus's journeys during his ministry. This facilitator training was developed with the Malaysia Baptist Theological Seminary (MBTS). When one book is finished, the facilitators

3. Jo Lane, "Serving the Chinese Diaspora," *GO Magazine* (July 2015): 10.

4. Shared by Jason Lee at the Increase conference "Empowering Churches, Equipping Disciples," Chiang Mai, 13–17 November 2017.

repeat the process until all six books of The Life of Christ are done, which takes up to eighteen months.

All the trained group leaders use the Leaders' Guide with questions and answers. The Leaders' Guide was developed by Jason and Jane as a supporting tool for group leaders. Altogether in ten years, they have trained thousands of qualified group leaders for The Life of Christ among Chinese churches in the diaspora. In fact, they have given out about 4,600 certificates! The TEE classes are now in twenty-five countries or areas: China (including Taiwan, Hong Kong, and Macau), USA, Malaysia, Indonesia, Australia, UK, Northern Ireland, Italy, Spain, Brunei, Myanmar, Thailand, Laos, Cambodia, Vietnam, Korea, Japan, Greece, Madagascar, Reunion Island, Ecuador, and Hungary.[5]

Inspired to Impact Others[6]

One of the students, Brother Ju, came to a TEE class when he had only been a believer for little more than a year. He had studied Abundant Life, and his life changed noticeably. Then he joined The Life of Christ training and took a year and a half to finish. The moment he finished, he wanted to be a group facilitator of the course. So nowadays not only is his life changed by the word of God through this course, he has also blessed and made an impact on many people in his surrounding area.

Brother Ju used to be a very high ranking government official, and his wife was not happy with him. But God changed him, and now he serves God everywhere – together with his wife! He has facilitated about sixteen classes in just three years, which means he has taught 183 graduates. He has introduced the courses to so many areas, and the church leaders really like it. Spiritually speaking, Brother Ju was only young, but with the TEE training, he was equipped so deeply and quickly that he was able to affect many people around him.

---

5. Lane, "Serving the Chinese Diaspora."

6. The content in this section was shared at the Increase conference "Exploring New Horizons," Kuala Lumpur, 20–25 April 2015.

This passion for sharing the new-found truths through TEE courses is not unique. There are many such testimonies. One is from a believer who was originally from Nanjing. He says,

> I was a confused Christian. One night I couldn't sleep – I just had the thought that I had to take seminary class. That was where I encountered TEE. When I started studying, I knew this was for me. I learned to remember the Scripture passage from Matthew 9: the crop is ripe, but there are not enough workers. That was God's calling for me, and I had a strong desire to share these things. I went to my own church in Nanjing – I had never been a farmer, but when I read God's word, I felt I had to bring TEE to my home town.

God Loves the Chinese Church[7]

TEE is used a lot in house churches. One pastor of a house church who received intensive training from Jason and Jane said,

> Through this great tool, we know that God loves the Chinese church and that he chooses us. We know we are not worthy, but The Life of Christ courses have built up our life. The Bible is no longer theory; it has become a life application to trust God in everything and to be like Christ and love people. Though my education level is low, you have always encouraged me so I could finish. I am very grateful.

Another house church leader from Wenzhou says, "We had never seen something so easy and simple yet so detailed and profound. It is excellent for training church leaders. This is my vision, and I am so happy and grateful we can use TEE." His experience is shared by many other pastors and leaders. One of them wrote that he was encouraged through the use of TEE. He says, "My

---

7. The content in this section is from various testimonies by Jason and Jane Lee at Increase Conferences between 2010 and 2017. They do not give the names of the pastors for security reasons.

first impression was how easy the materials seemed. But the more I studied this, the more I realized how much we needed to focus on the foundations. The learning is very deep, and the method very simple. It works so well for lay people. Besides, it is good for church growth and very helpful for ministers."

Chinese TEE in Malaysia

As mentioned in chapter 14, the Malaysia Baptist Theological Seminary (MBTS) includes The Life of Christ series in their Chinese-medium bachelor's program which is accredited by the Asia Theological Association. Dr Mooi Sai Lim, Associate Dean at MBTS, was looking for Bible courses for the seminary that can be taught in churches as well. So she was very interested in The Life of Christ courses. She says,

> I joined the class and thought it was very good and helpful. It looked very simple, yet the knowledge is deep. After going through the six books, I have a clear picture of Jesus's life and ministry. Many of our students, some are pastors, started classes at their church, and some helped other churches to teach their members. I have started three classes at my church, and my students shared with me that their church members have experienced change in their life after taking this course. We have the Leaders' Guide as well, so that students can become teachers, too. In this way more and more Christians will study The Life of Christ in different churches, and their lives will change.[8]

Pray and Connect

Please pray
- for health and strength for Jason and Jane Lee as they travel and train around the world;
- for churches and Christians in China to continue to grow despite facing new pressures from their government;

---

8. Dr Mooi Sai Lim, email to Graham Aylett.

- for many more Chinese churches in the diaspora to take up TEE as a tool for discipleship.

TEE Movers for the Chinese Church
General enquiries: teetmcc@gmail.com

ARAB WORLD

24

Arab World Developing Leaders for Church Growth

Hanna-Ruth van Wingerden

Background[1]

What is known as the Arab world comprises twenty-two countries stretching from the Arabian Peninsula in the east across the northern parts of Africa in the west that are members of the Arab League. These countries have a combined population of around 422 million people, over half of whom are under twenty-five years of age. The majority are Muslim, and Islam has official status in most countries. There are Christian churches with a very long history in this part of the world, especially in Egypt, Syria, Lebanon, Iraq, Jordan, and Israel, and the Palestinian territories. The Coptic Church in Egypt is the largest body of believers in the region.

Throughout the region, there are huge differences in people and countries. While some countries partly observe the strict Sharia law, others have a secular legal system. Some countries are wealthy due to natural resources like oil; other countries are struggling with poverty. The region is colored by conflict,

---

1. The facts in this section are from "Arab World," Wikipedia, https://en.wikipedia.org/wiki/Arab_world, accessed August 2018.

especially now in Syria, and huge numbers of refugees are scattered throughout neighboring countries. All these factors add to the challenges of the church in this part of the world.

TEE in the Arab World

The Program for Theological Education by Extension (PTEE) provides TEE resources in the Arab world. The vision of PTEE is to develop leaders through theological education by extension for the growth of the church and the positive transformation of society in the Arab world. They seek to help church members grow in their understanding of the Bible and to make Christ known in this part of the world. PTEE works with and through local churches to develop indigenous leaders for the local churches. PTEE also serves Arabic speakers living in the Arab diaspora including Europe, North America, and Australia. PTEE and Increase are closely connected. PTEE's Director, Jiries Habash, is a member of the Increase Committee. E-learning Director Rick Weymouth also serves as an Increase Equipper, and he helps with all matters digital.

In 1981 in Amman, Jordan, representatives from Middle Eastern church denominations and Christian organizations established PTEE. The main goal was to provide theological education at the bachelor's level for leaders in the church. By 2006, course facilitators had been trained in at least nine different countries. PTEE works in each country through a national committee. The long-term goal is to have PTEE classes offered in all the countries of the Arab World. At the moment, PTEE holds about forty classes per year, serving nearly two hundred students. Beginning in 2018, PTEE began offering BA courses online which makes PTEE courses more accessible and more flexible for students across the region. This online program also makes life a lot easier for PTEE as it is a challenge for one organization to serve all of these countries.[2]

---

2. "PTEE History," http://ptee.org/eng/ptee-history/, accessed July 2018.

Who Benefits from PTEE?[3]

Ra'ed from Algeria came across PTEE through its website, and he reached out to PTEE to learn how he could bring theological training to his church. Like most believers in Algeria, Ra'ed came to Christ from the country's national religion. He is teaching full time at his university and pursuing his PhD, but he is also responsible for Christian education for more than three hundred members of his church.

Ra'ed's church has no trained pastor, so he and the other elders serve as ministry leaders according to their spiritual gifts. They all work full time in addition to voluntarily serving the church, all without any formal theological training. Their Bible knowledge and leadership skills are the result of self-study and experience. These men, along with other local church leaders, need and desire theological training. Without theological training in sound doctrine, there is a danger of false teaching coming into the churches.

Both Ra'ed and his wife as well as others in his church are taking PTEE online courses to increase their Bible knowledge. A good knowledge of the Bible and the teachings of Jesus is so important in his context because many people are young in faith and not many Christians have theological training. Apart from the danger of false teachings, Bible knowledge is important because many Christians struggle with persecution from their families and society. One of the big issues that new believers struggle with is the question of who Jesus is. Is he really the Son of God? Or is he just a prophet? It is very important for every believer to know how to answer questions about this pivotal point.

Sana is a good example of how the resources of the PTEE are helping people to stay faithful despite oppression, and helping others grow in Christ as well. Sana is a forty-five-year-old follower of Jesus. She is a wife and mother, a Sunday school teacher, a youth teacher, and a theology student with PTEE. She was introduced to Christianity by her husband, who helped her to compare the status of women in her culture with the status of women in the Bible. Sana began to question her Muslim religion. However, as with so many Muslims, she still could not believe that the man Jesus is the Son of God, that he is divine.

---

3. The testimonies in this section were selected from PTEE updates and personal conversations and shared by Jiries Habash at the Increase conference "Empowering Churches, Equipping Disciples," Chiang Mai, 13–17 November 2017.

When Sana reluctantly attended a church Christmas party with her husband, she was struck by the warmth and love these Christians had for each other. She had never experienced anything like it! Sana finally went to a church prayer meeting and realized that these people had something she did not possess. She prayed to know the truth, and God answered Sana's prayer in a dream. As a result, she gave her life to the Lord, accepting Jesus as her Savior. Then Sana understood that she needed to know the word of God so she could give an answer for the hope she has.

Sana's first course with PTEE was on the Book of Acts, and she has now completed six courses. Sana and her husband continue to live in a Muslim neighborhood which, as an outspoken follower of Jesus, presents both opportunities and challenges. She faces ongoing discrimination in her community, and her children are constantly put under pressure by their teachers to abandon Christianity. Sana explained that she needs to know the word of God deeply so that she can answer the challenges and questions posed by her neighbors and co-workers.

Armed with the biblical knowledge she is gaining through her PTEE courses, Sana continues to be a light in her part of the world. She serves in her church each week in the Sunday school and is even using the TEE course Abundant Life with the older teenagers. According to Sana, teaching the children and youth is a challenge. For this reason, Sana is committed to increasing her knowledge of the Bible. As a result of taking the PTEE class Book of Romans, she was able to teach and clearly explain "justification" and "salvation" and what these theological concepts mean to the teenagers in their personal life.

Sonya is from Syria. As a women's Bible study leader, youth teacher, and worship leader, Sonya embodies the vision and mission of PTEE. Despite the challenges of a civil war, no electricity, and travel risks, she graduated with a bachelor of theology through the PTEE program in 2016. Since graduating, she and her husband have trained as PTEE course facilitators and have begun to lead classes in three places in Syria. So far, Sonya has facilitated nine PTEE classes. She shared that while she was studying the Christian Counselling course, her neighbors were planning to divorce. After praying with the wife and sharing biblical counselling, the woman accepted Christ, became close to the Lord, and did not allow the divorce to happen. Instead, she has become a light to her family and looks to the Bible for guidance.

Victor from Egypt has a heart for the Nubian people. Nubians are found in Sudan and southern Egypt, and they trace their roots to the early inhabitants of the central Nile valley, believed to be one of the earliest cradles of civilization. Centuries ago, the Nubian people were Christian, but most were converted to Islam in the fifteenth and sixteenth centuries. It is very difficult to reach these people, but then Victor found that medical outreach opens doors to them.

The team that Victor leads visits about twenty villages each week. They run a number of different community development programs: languages, women's rights, medical clinics, and basic literacy. Victor's team asks what is needed and then they try to deliver it. This outreach to the Nubian people has been going on for five years. What started with a small group of just four baptized Christians studying Arabic TEE materials is now making a real impact. A good number of people have come to Christ and are interested in reading the Bible – or perhaps listen to the audio Bible. Technology helps! It especially helps Muslim women, because while they are listening, no one knows they are listening to the word of God.

Victor's work has not gone unnoticed, and the team has had visits from the secret police. But Victor feels compelled: "We HAVE to do it." By law people can choose their religion in Egypt, but this is not true in practice.

In Conclusion

Since the beginning of PTEE, nearly three thousand students have attended over 1,300 classes, and there have been 115 facilitator training workshops. Through on location and online classes, PTEE is helping people like Ra'ed, Sana, Sonya, and Victor to shine in this region. PTEE provides evangelical theological education to Arabic speakers wherever they live in the Arab world to advance the kingdom, build the church, and transform society. Today, PTEE is beginning work among Arabic-speaking churches in Northern Africa, and continues to work to expand its presence and impact across the Arab world.

Pray and Connect

Please pray

- for PTEE to expand its reach and impact for the advancement of the kingdom across the Arab world;
- for the safety of Arabic-speaking believers in the Arab world;
- that the Holy Spirit will open doors for PTEE across this unreached part of the world;
- for PTEE staff, national committees, class facilitators, and students who seek to build and strengthen the church and transform Arab society.

Program for Theological Education by Extension
General enquires: pteeinfo@ptee.org
Website: http://www.ptee.org
PTEE news: Kristyn Kuhlman at kuhlman@ptee.org

Channels of Transformation

The vast majority of TEE learners in Asia do not work full time in churches but in ordinary jobs. They can influence their workplaces and neighborhoods. This section includes three examples in which transformed individuals went on to bring transformation in their settings, at least to some extent.

CAMBODIA

25

Cambodia
Holistic Mission

Penelope Vinden and Graham Aylett

Background[1]

Cambodia is a tropical country in Southeast Asia with a mix of low-lying plains, uplands, and low mountains. The population of just over 16 million is concentrated in the southeast, particularly in and around the capital of Phnom Penh. Although Cambodia has experienced strong economic growth over the past decade, it remains one of the poorest countries in Asia, and long-term growth is challenged by corruption, limited human resources, income inequality, and lack of good job prospects. Over 90 percent of Cambodians are ethnically Khmer and practice Buddhism.

Operation World speaks of "unprecedented and unexpected church growth over the last twenty years. From only a few thousand Christians surviving into the 1990s, believers may now top 3.5 percent of the population. This growth is almost entirely through church multiplication, and done by indigenous church planters and evangelists." Some of the greatest growth in Cambodia has been among the smaller ethnic groups where people have little education. TEE

---

1. The information in this section is from "Cambodia," Operation World, http://www. operationworld.org/country/camb/owtext.html, accessed August 2018; and "Cambodia," Lonely Planet, https://www.lonelyplanet.com/cambodia, accessed August 2018.

courses provide a way to train leaders, teach doctrine, and apply biblical truths to everyday life in this context.

Although the church in Cambodia is growing, many pastors lack training, and there is a limited range of Christian literature. Being a Christian, while legal, still requires people to stand firm against a culture of which Buddhism is an integral part. Converting to Christianity is often seen as a betrayal of family, friends, and culture. In 2017, the prime minister met with 2,500 church leaders and called for the country not to harass Christians but to let them meet freely.

TEE in Cambodia

An article in the SEAN newsletter *SPREAD* describes how TEE came to Cambodia and how it has been used:[2]

> The story of SEAN materials in Khmer, the national language of Cambodia begins with an Alliance missionary, Paul Ellison. He grew up in Cambodia, the son of one of the earliest Protestant missionaries, and he had excellent Khmer language. Later, while living in the States during the 1980s, he translated the six books of the Compendium on his own! He and others used them to train Cambodian pastors in the States. The Life of Christ was then used in Cambodian refugee camps in Thailand and was also used when the first Alliance Cambodian pastors returned to Cambodia in the early 1990s.
>
> The Alliance in Cambodia has planted a denomination called the Khmer Evangelical Church, or KEC. The KEC has TEE built into its DNA in a very intentional way. The Constitution states that any elder must have studied TEE, or be studying TEE, or something similar.
>
> A senior leader in the denomination commented: "We used the TEE program as a foundation for our training. We have these study centres – that's really where we get our pastors from. This

---

2. "Cambodia," *SPREAD*, SEAN International, April 2016, 2–3, https://www.seaninternational.com/news/2016/SPREAD_2016_4-r2.pdf.

is our strategy. We can plant churches anywhere, but if we don't have this program to strengthen them, they won't be strong. I really believe this is a very important program."

Over the course of time within the KEC, about a thousand people have gone through the two-year leadership training level.

TEE as a Church Planting and Training Tool

The SPREAD article goes on to describe TEE use in Cambodia:[3]

> In 2003, a C&MA medical family were available to serve in Cambodia. The decision was made to send them as part of a team to the darkest place in Cambodia. This was Poipet, which the Lonely Planet Guide introduces as "Long the armpit of Cambodia, notorious for its squalor, scams and sleaze . . ." In 2003 there were no churches, and no hospital. The team of one doctor, two nurses, someone with training in emergency medical services, and an experienced church-planting couple began to work to meet physical and spiritual needs, with the TEE program as their church planting and training tool. Today, there is a hospital, and eight churches. The missionaries have made the decision to leave, because the churches can stand on their own feet now. Praise God!

TEE in a Rural Village[4]

Oeuy and Chathan moved to the United States from Cambodia as part of the flood of refugees that left Southeast Asia in the 1970s and 80s. Ten years ago in 2008, they moved back to Cambodia, relocating to a tiny village. TEE is ideal in their context where few people are educated. Oeuy says, "The thing I like best about TEE is its simple design. There is group discussion; there are

---

3. "Cambodia," *SPREAD*, 3.

4. The content in this section is from Chathan and Oeuy interviewed by Penny Vinden at the Increase conference "Empowering Churches, Equipping Disciples," Chiang Mai, 13–17 November 2017.

questions prepared for you to ask; they give you small amounts of information little by little; and there is time to talk about application. For me – I learn a lot with this methodology!"

A major problem in Cambodia is the destruction of natural resources. While large parts of the country are designated as nature reserves, boundaries are not always respected, and for most of this century, Cambodia has been one of the world's worst countries for deforestation. Oeuy and Chathan see their ministry as to the "whole person" – they are keen to apply Scriptural principles that people learn in TEE to everyday life, including the care of creation.

> At first it was very hard moving to this tiny place. People have so little. They have no toilets but just go into the jungle, and the pigs follow them all the time. Also it was hard for our older children – we had a teenage girl and a boy almost a teenager, as well as a four year old. So one of the first things we did was to build a toilet. But then the people laughed at us for using it! They laughed at us for everything at first. But later when they saw how easy many things were for us, they wanted to do the same things, too. Now everyone has an outdoor toilet!
>
> But it isn't just about the toilets. They have a lot of pigs who eat and destroy everything. So the people walk several kilometres through the jungle to make their fields where the pigs won't destroy them. But we showed them they can keep the pigs under control with fences, so they can grow things very close to home. And they are growing more nutritious things too, and raising chickens and ducks so they have more protein in their diet. This means they are healthier and also have more free time to do other things. We have a pastor now who is able to travel and do evangelism three days a week, knowing that there is enough food for his wife and children while he is gone. Before, the wife would complain if the husband left her. We are just maximising the resources God has given us.
>
> Some people from other villages come and ask us, "Why is your village so clean and so green?" And we say Jesus changed our hearts, Jesus changed our place. And then they say, "Come and help us." And as soon as we start working on a project with them,

they see that they can do it. And soon they also say, "We want to study what God tells us to do; we want to do what God tells us."

We are so close to his creation. We can see that God is there all the time. He has given us rain, the land – it is up to us to identify all the resources around us and be good stewards, depending on God to provide.

New TEE Courses for Cambodia

One of the exciting things happening in TEEAC right now is the development of a TEE course about the spirit world. One of the TEEAC members is taking part in the Increase Course Writing Training. (Read more about this in chapter 30.) The fear of spirits and demons is real and leads Cambodians to try to appease those spirits in order to get protection or to get power and influence. Consequently, people are being deceived and live in bondage to those spirits. This TEE course aims to help believers live in the freedom won for them by the victory of Jesus. In addition to the course on the spirit world, a course on holistic ministry is also being developed.

Pray and Connect

Please pray
- for Oeuy, Chathan, Moch and Miranda (missionary workers in Cambodia) as they work as a team to write the course on the spirit world;
- that this course will bless many Christians in Cambodia;
- for the leadership of TEEAC;
- for the center study leaders;
- for financial resources to serve the churches effectively.

TEE Association of Cambodia
General enquiries: edteeac@gmail.com
Facebook: https://www.facebook.com/TEEac-335787733225556/

JACK'S STORY

with ML Low

It started as any other day. But suddenly I heard a voice say, "You have to go to church."

Instinctively I replied, "Why?" I was born into a typical Buddhist family in Laos, and church was never on my mind.

The voice did not leave me alone. Not long after, I heard the same command again, "You have to go to church!"

I argued, "Why do I have to go to church?" There was already a stirring and a softening in my heart. When the voice spoke for the third time later that day, I did not fight back. I replied, "OK, I will go!" That agreement to go to church was also the moment I decided to follow Christ. A great sense of joy then descended on me. It was a totally new feeling that I had never felt before.

As a new person in church, I did not know how to pray. When people sang, I followed along. I raised my hands to worship, and the Holy Spirit touched me. There was a great sense of peace and a burst of new energy within me. I also had this new strong desire to know Jesus intimately.

I was very excited with my new faith. Everything I said was either about Jesus or the church. My family thought I had gone crazy. On the day of my baptism, my family was so upset that they took away my motorbike. But nothing could deter me – I walked all the way to my baptism venue. The more my family tried to stop me from going to church, the more I prayed and served. One day, my father was so angry that he chased me out of our home.

Upon my graduation from university, I chose to be a church volunteer. Every day I followed my pastor to preach, teach, visit, and pray for people. I enjoyed learning all that Jesus has commanded us to do.

Within my family, God has performed multiple miracles. I am very thankful that both my parents are now believers. My father accepted Christ after he was delivered from a demonic attack. My mother came to Christ after she had a stroke. A number of my siblings and family members have also accepted Jesus after experiencing his healing in their lives.

Jesus's Great Commission is to "go and make disciples of all nations, baptizing them in the name of the Father and of the Son and of the Holy Spirit" (Matthew 28:19). We are just beginning to use TEE courses in Laos, and I think they will be a very good tool to disciple the believers. I am very excited about the potential impact of TEE on our people.

RUSSIA

26

Russia
Hope in the Midst
of Challenges

Hanna-Ruth van Wingerden

Background[1]

Russia spans no less than eleven time zones, and stretches from Europe to North Korea. This country is big! The inhabitants are as diverse as the country's wildlife and climate. Russia has a population of about 150 million composed of over 190 nationalities, the majority being ethnic Russians. However, some of the other indigenous groups are quite large; for example, there are over 5.5 million Tatars. There are fifteen cities in Russia with over one million people, and the largest cities are Moscow and St. Petersburg. There are also big cities in the east, like Novosibirsk, Vladivostok, and Irkutsk. Nevertheless, quite a number of people live in remote small towns and villages.

Although Russia is rich in natural resources like oil and gas, these riches do not flow to the average citizen. Poverty has always been present, at first for most people in the countryside serving the nobility and later under the communist

---

1. The information in this section is from "Russia," Wikipedia, https://en.wikipedia.org/wiki/Russia, accessed July 2018.

system, and for many people, things became worse with the disintegration of the Soviet Union in 1991.

Politics and religion have always been closely intertwined. When Prince Vladimir converted to Christianity in the tenth century, Christianity became the official religion, and the Russian Orthodox Church became the dominant religious force. Under Soviet rule, faith of any kind was discouraged and most churches forbidden. When the Soviet Union dissolved, the Orthodox Church was once again viewed as one of the major elements in Russian culture. This situation can be a challenge for ethnic minorities who hold different religious beliefs, like Muslims. Vladimir Putin is closely connected with the Orthodox Church, strengthening the idea that Orthodox Christianity is an essential part of Russia and the Russian people.

This mix of religion and politics makes for a lot of mistrust towards the church. There are small numbers of Protestants in Russia, and since 1991, many missionaries have come to Russia and other post-Soviet countries. Recently, legislation banning religious meetings anywhere but in officially registered church buildings has threatened many Protestant groups. This legislation makes church home groups, cell groups, and TEE groups illegal if they are meeting outside of a registered building.

TEE in Russia

The Russian TEE program called ORTA has faced serious challenges; but praise God, at least one section of its ministries, Printing and Distributing TEE and SEAN Study Materials, managed to obtain registration. The ORTA TEE program was established in the far east of the Russian Federation nearly fifteen years ago and has spread westwards with groups now studying in many regions. Under SEAN's generous license agreement, ORTA's team has translated and adapted a number of TEE courses specifically for nurturing new believers, motivating, training and equipping disciples, and leadership training. The International Director of ORTA, Anneta Vysotskaya, is Chair of the Increase Committee and has an important role in supporting and encouraging development of TEE in Central Asia.

Transformation

Within Russian culture lies a truly rich tapestry of art, literature, and music. The people tend to be very generous and hospitable. However, one of the social issues in Russia is the large number of people living with addiction to alcohol and drugs. This problem impacts many lives and many families. Unemployment is high, and even people who have jobs live on low wages which leads to feelings of hopelessness. One way of finding relief is grabbing the bottle or the drugs, which leads to further unemployment but also to domestic abuse, broken families, and high divorce rates.

Nina, a woman on the Russian TEE team, can testify to the hope she found in a desperate situation. Nina is now part of the group leader training team, but she used to be a drug addict. She was sentenced to nine years in prison for drug dealing, but by God's grace, she spent only two and a half months there. She called out to God in prison, but when she was released, she found it very difficult to change her life around and got into trouble again and again. Finally she got so scared that she decided to find a church. She then became part of a small group studying Abundant Life. Nina says,

> Thanks to the studies, I was brought to a true repentance and began growing in the Lord. A few years later, I was fasting and asking God what ministry he would call me to. In a few days, I was going somewhere by bus, and a woman sat next to me. She was studying a TEE group leader's manual carefully. As it turned out, she led TEE groups in the church, and she said I would also be able to lead groups after training. So I got trained in a group leader workshop. I shared this news with the pastor of my church in Ussuriisk, and he told me to run a group at the rehabilitation center. At weekends I used to go there to lead the group. I have now been a TEE group leader in the rehabilitation center for three years. The students in this group are not only men from the rehabilitation center but also people from the church. Later some students in the group became TEE group leaders.[2]

---

2. Tamara Kulesh, ORTA Russian Director, shared Nina's testimony at the Increase conference "Empowering Churches, Equipping Disciples," Chiang Mai, 13–17 November 2017.

Other team members call Nina one of the most dedicated people in the group leader training team because she's always willing to go to places no matter how far away. They say, "She is such a good example of how God can transform people through TEE. In a matter of years, Nina went from being a mess in all the areas of her life to being a minister who trains people to train others."[3]

Building Churches[4]

People being trained leads to more growth and to churches being blessed. People have shared that TEE courses do not just help the students but also the people around them. The materials are good and easy to understand. They give people the ability to preach the gospel, and group members learn to answer peoples' questions in simple ways. As for ministers, the courses help them to prepare their sermons. Now sermons are not just about salvation; they are about being disciples.

Dmitry is the pastor of a church on Sakhalin Island, an island in the far east of Russia, just north of Japan. He says,

> I was the only trainee from our church. I am now leading an Abundant Life group of eight students in our church. We have a cell G-12 church and have been using the Alpha Course for a number of years, so we are familiar with small group activities. TEE has proved to suit our church structure ideally as a systematic way to educate our members. This was just like a missing piece in the puzzle. In my opinion, ORTA can be easily built into other church structures as well, because it is a program that anyone can use.

Pastor Dmitry continues to explain that Abundant Life is not only a great tool to teach new believers, it is also a great tool for more mature disciples.

> As simple as it is, it motivates even "old spiritual dinosaurs," creating a new excitement in them to study and apply Scripture.

---

3. Kulesh, 2017.
4. The content in this section is from ORTA Annual Reports 2015 and 2016.

In my own experience, after we studied the lesson on reading the Bible, I gained a new zeal to read and study the word of God for myself, and not just because I have to do it as a pastor in my sermon preparation. TEE presents the essential information for a Christian in a concise and systematic way, but it goes far beyond just increasing the knowledge. It really encourages the students to apply it in their lives.

Oleg is a member of The Living Faith Church, and he agrees with Pastor Dmitry.

When we study the TEE courses, we are growing, confirming our faith, and learning to witness to others about Christ. We find it easier to understand the Bible. This program helps people to relax. They make friends with each other and start helping others. They start to think and understand life in a Christian way. And this is really Abundant Life! People in my group led their non-believing spouses and children to God. Some started to have better marriage relationships. Many were able to discover their potential during these studies. The program is also wonderful because it does not touch any denominational questions. It can be used everywhere. The knowledge that we receive can be applied in our life.

Looking Ahead

Being a small team in the largest country on earth, there is a lot of work to be done. But it is getting done! New groups are formed and new trainers trained each year. At the moment, 1,400 students are studying in more than two hundred groups. The group leader training team has run 104 group leader training seminars and trained more than 1,500 group leaders.

Because of the great distances involved, it is challenging for trainers based in the far east of Russia to serve the whole country. The formation of regional teams has been an important part of the growth of the program. Please pray for these teams, that the Lord would give them energy and vision not only to serve their regions, but also to catalyze the formation of new regional teams.

One of the aims the team is working towards is to obtain a state license for ORTA's educational work. This license will help to legally protect the ORTA team, TEE students, and churches and also to provide valid educational certificates and diplomas to ORTA students in Russia and potentially in other countries.

The Russian TEE team also has a strong vision to serve Russian-speaking churches wherever they are in the world. For example in December 2017, the Uzbek TEE team and ORTA trained new group leaders in Seoul, South Korea, and the number of groups and students is growing there. Read more about this development in chapter 12.

Pray and Connect

Please pray
- for God's protection over ORTA, TEE groups, and group leaders meeting across Russia;
- for good health and energy for the ORTA team, including the regional teams;
- for ORTA's vision to reach out to Russian speakers across the world.

ORTA
General enquiries: Tamara Kulesh, ORTA Russian Director
tamaravladk@gmail.com

A TEE group studying Abundant Light in Russian

SOUTH KOREA

27

South Korea Transformation Through Discipleship

Graham Aylett and Hanna-Ruth van Wingerden

Background[1]

South Korea lies on the southern half of the Korean Peninsula. North and South Korea have been separated since 1953. Whereas North Korea went under a strict communist regime, South Korea eventually became a democracy with an elected president. The economy of South Korea has been booming since the early 1960s when the country became greatly industrialized with a focus on new technologies.

South Korea enjoys freedom of religion, and approximately one third of the people are Christians. Over time, many religions have influenced the South Koreans including shamanism, Buddhism, Taoism, and Confucianism. All of these have left their traces. For example, the values of Confucianism are still influencing Korean daily life and family relationships, and Buddhism is still prominent, even among people who may be nominally Christian.

---

1. The information in this section is from "South Korea," Wikipedia, https://en.wikipedia.org/wiki/South_Korea, accessed September 2018; and "South Korea," Encyclopaedia Britannica, https://www.britannica.com/place/South-Korea, accessed September 2018.

TEE in South Korea

Many Korean churches have a commitment to prayer and fasting and are well-structured and organized. When such churches embrace TEE, there can be real transformation! For some church leaders, the growth of the church in whatever way possible has been very important, but for a growing group, attitudes are starting to change. TEE can help these churches to grow in knowledge of the word of God. Many church members have also found that the methods of TEE, doing Bible study in small groups at home, is much easier to fit into a busy lifestyle than long sessions in the church.

The Korean church as a whole has a remarkable missionary vision. "South Korea has sent out 27,436 missionaries in 2017, second only to the United States."[2] They are reaching "over 170 countries throughout the world with nearly more than 65 percent serving in parts of Asia."[3] When TEE is introduced to these Korean missionaries as a tool for church planting, discipleship, and leadership training, many take it and use it and are seeing much fruit.

Two organizations serve the church with TEE materials: TEE Korea and Korea TEE Ministries (KTEE). Starting in the early 2000s, the ministry of these two organizations has grown tremendously and together they reach many thousands of Korean students in thousands of churches in Korea and beyond.

TEE Korea

TEE Korea has developed a special emphasis on all church members learning together and has given this approach the name TEE Community Learning (TEECL). TEE Korea challenges church leaders to embrace a vision based on Colossians 1:28, "He is the one we proclaim, admonishing and teaching everyone with all wisdom, *so that we may present everyone mature in Christ.*" TEE Korea has an extensive program of courses to help ordinary church members grow towards maturity in Christ. TEE Korea works with Korean churches in South Korea and also in other countries. They have equipped TEE leaders in Central Asia, Japan, India, the Philippines, and Indonesia, and especially in Indonesia have helped to foster a national TEE team. For a number

---

2. Joel Kim, "Which Country Sends the [Second] Most Missionaries?" *Challies*, 21 February 2018.
3. Kim, "Which Country Sends."

of years, TEE Korea Director Stephen Cho was a member of the Increase Committee. He is also an Increase Equipper and has travelled to a number of countries introducing Community Learning TEE, providing expertise, and training group leaders.

Transformation through TEE Community Learning[4]

People may come to church for years but still do not actively follow Jesus in their daily lives. As one Korean pastor comments, "Many church members say, 'I believe,' and they attend church. But that's all there is to it, no more." Even people in leadership roles may not know their Bible well. One shared, "I became a believer many years ago and considered myself mature in faith. But my Bible knowledge was disordered and mixed up."

But the TEE Community Learning program is bringing transformation to individuals and churches across Korea and beyond. The leader above continued, "But, during the TEE seminar, I came to clearly understand the message of the Bible. This brought great joy to me!"

In order to better understand what God is really doing through the systematic study of his word, TEE Korea conducted a survey.[5] They found that 97 percent of TEE students said that they were changed through the courses, and nearly 85 percent were able to make a connection between the word of God and their own daily lives.

The pastor of Samchun Methodist Church sees these changes and connections happening in his congregation. "People now understand the word of God, and they have found the will of God for themselves," he shares. In Yewoorim Church, there is a greater sense of unity since people started the courses, and people care for each other much more than before. Also, the people in the courses have become more active in evangelism, and the vast majority of new students have become regular members of the church. It's not

---

4. The quotes from unnamed church pastors in this section are from the brochure "TEE Community Learning" by TEE Korea, 2013.

5. The survey results were presented by Dr Cho Sung Rae to the Increase conference "Empowering Churches, Equipping Disciples," Chiang Mai, 13–17 November 2017.

only the church members who are changed. "I know I have changed as I've been involved," said the pastor of Yewoorim Church.

The pastor of Chechun Glory Church is impressed by the transformation he has seen. Through the systematic Bible education TEECL provides, members have a deeper understanding of the word of God. And the group sessions have helped to bring a culture of mature discussion in the church. Even the preaching on Sunday is not a one-way street anymore but involves active discussion. One of the great results is that the pastor and church members have learned to communicate better, and this communication has made the whole church much healthier both spiritually and emotionally. The survey also showed that around 75 percent of students said TEE helped them improve relationships and helped create a better atmosphere in their church.

The pastor of Yoosung Church also recognizes these improved relationships and says, "The sharing during studies really helps members to understand each other." In Samchun Methodist Church, they found that the community learning has brought a sense of companionship and a spiritual unity to church members.

Serving the Army

South Korea is officially still in a state of war with North Korea, and every young man has to do two years of military service. "TEE Korea has been working to disciple believers in military bases with TEE materials for the past 14 years. At least 15,000 soldiers, officers (both high and low ranking) and their spouses have studied at least one course. Now it has become . . . a near self-sustaining programme."[6] One of the soldiers said,

> I was in a Bible study group using TEE courses when I was doing my military service. I finished both Abundant Life and Abundant Light during my conscription. I appreciate these materials so much, as they gave me the chance to hear the good news. I will never forget the first time I confessed that I was a child of God through your book.[7]

---

6. "South Korea," *SPREAD,* November 2016, 2.
7. "Testimony from South Korea . . . 'Hello, my name is Jake Lim . . . ,'" *SPREAD,* April 2018.

This young soldier may well have been connected to a TEE study group through one of his officers, because not only soldiers but also army officers help the spread of TEE. Senior officers and their spouses are involved in this ministry as coordinators or small group leaders. One of the results is the improvement of the military's leadership strength. It is safe to say that these factors are contributing to a fertile atmosphere for spreading the gospel in the military.

KTEE Ministries

"KTEE Ministries works with local churches in South Korea as well as Korean diaspora churches and mission fields all over the world."[8] Over the last sixteen years, God has used KTEE Ministries to strengthen Korean churches and support Korean missionaries in many places. In 3,596 Extension Centers, 25,000 men and women have taken KTEE courses. In addition, most of the SEAN materials were translated and published in Korean. KTEE Ministries is flourishing in the United States, Canada, Japan, the Philippines, China, Thailand, Vietnam, and Australia, but now mainly focuses on India and the Philippines.[9]

> KTEE Ministries also work with a Christian enterprise 'E-land' and its chaplains. E-land is one of the top 50 companies in Korea. They have 15,000 employees in Korea, 30,000 in China as well as 30 affiliates and 60 chaplains who are working diligently to train and equip employees with biblical values.[10]

Je-Ju Vision Church

Je-Ju Island is the largest island off the coast of the Korean peninsula. Its location in the south and its pleasant climate and beautiful nature make it

---

8. "South Korea," *SPREAD*, 3.

9. From a presentation at the Increase conference "Empowering Churches, Equipping Disciples," November 2017.

10. "South Korea," *SPREAD*, 3.

an attraction for tourists. Its nickname is the Hawaii of Korea, and Chinese tourists have called it the island of the gods. "In the past the area was strongly influenced by the occult, superstition and local evil spirits,"[11] and shamanism was one of the main practices.

> In the early stages of planting a church there, Pastor Jigyun Shin came into contact with TEE. He started the SEAN course, The Life of Christ, with ten people. Some were middle school or high school graduates. One was 60 years old. Six of them completed the whole of The Life of Christ course.
>
> A major advance in discipleship training in the church followed. Fifty more students started The Life of Christ. Tutors were trained to lead other SEAN courses such as Abundant Life and Abundant Light (The Big Picture). In all, 150 people completed those courses. Now even more are taking the courses.
>
> Je-Ju Vision Church has proved that TEE is an excellent tool for discipleship, evangelism and church growth.[12]

Age, education, and gender do not matter. Any church member or believer can grow through these courses.

> As a result of this growth, the church has purchase a church building owned by Sung An Church, which was the very first church planted there and is one of the largest in Je-Ju Island.
>
> Pastor Shin says, "Our members, who have been trained by TEE, are well equipped to lead any small group they are assigned to. I am free to do other things for the church as well as members, because our group leaders can take care of the things that I used to do."[13]

---

11. "Je-Ju Vision Church: An Excellent Example of Discipleship for Rural and Island Churches," *SPREAD*, September 2010, 2.
12. "Je-Ju Vision Church," 3.
13. "Je-Ju Vision Church," 3.

Seoul Young Dong Church

Life in the big city is completely different from life in rural areas like Je-Ju Island. In Korea's capital Seoul,

> Some members of Young Dong Church are lawyers and high-ranking government employees.
>
> A challenge facing the church was how to train such busy people. A senior pastor searched for a way of training them so that they could influence people in their workplaces. TEE was an answer to his quest.
>
> Many were trained through the TEE program and they started leading TEE-supported small groups in their workplaces.
>
> Senior Pastor Chung Hyun Goo said, "There are things to which a senior pastor must go, or things with which people must come to the pastor, or things which a senior pastor must do. However, those who were trained by TEE are doing many of the things which a senior pastor used to do. They are building a church where they work and I am very proud of them."[14]

One of the core areas for KTEE overseas is the Philippines.

> In the Philippines, Korean diaspora, trained and equipped by TEE, now reaches out to local pastors. Many Korean foreign correspondents reside in Manila, the capital and we have come to realize that God already has prepared them to reach out to Filipinos, because they have no language barriers.
>
> One elder, Park Jin-Ho and his wife are currently training 50 Filipino pastors using SEAN materials. 10 of those pastors have graduated and, through their ministry, 175 new believers were baptized on Oct 2nd, 2016.[15]

---

14. "Seoul Young Dong Church sets an excellent example of discipleship for metropolitan area churches," *SPREAD*, September 2010, 3.
15. "South Korea," *SPREAD*, November 2016, 3.

Pray and Connect

Please pray
- for the Lord to use TEE to bring his transformation to many more Korean churches;
- for TEE Korea and KTEE Ministries as they reach out to other countries in Asia and beyond;
- for Korean missionaries to take up TEE and use it fruitfully in many places.

KTEE Ministries
Website: http://www.ktee.org
A detailed description of KTEE's history will be featured on the Increase Association website.

TEE Korea and TEE Community Learning
Website: http://www.teekorea.org

Part C

Innovation in TEE

Members of the Increase Committee
© ML Low. Used with permission.

28

Exploring New Horizons:
The Increase Association

Tim Green

The national TEE organizations in Asia are anchored in local soil. Led and governed within their own countries, they are not controlled from outside. So they decide their own priorities, raise their own funds, and choose or create their own courses in their own languages. This is a great strength.

However, this independence also tended to leave them isolated from wider contact and under-resourced. After all, they were using the same TEE method and often the same courses, and they were facing similar challenges and searching for solutions. But they did not know what other TEE movements were doing even in the next country. They had no forum where they could meet and share. This situation continued for decades.

Finally this gap began to be met by the Increase Association. Actually Increase started in 2006, when representatives of different training organizations came together with a vision for in-context leadership training for churches across the non-Western world. But by 2010, the focus turned to Asia, with Increase's conference in Nepal entitled "Twenty-First Century TEE in Asia: Challenges and Opportunities." This conference was the first time that most Asian TEE leaders had the chance to meet others from across the continent. It generated much energy leading to training workshops, the 2012 launch of new TEE programs across Central Asia, and a curriculum consultation in 2013.

At its 2015 conference, "Exploring New Horizons," Increase moved from being an informal network to an organized association of Asian church-based training organizations. Currently nearly all of these member bodies use TEE, but they do not have to. For instance the Hasat program in Turkey uses a different approach but shares the same vision and ethos. New members joined Increase at its 2017 conference, "Empowering Churches, Equipping Disciples," which was attended by nearly 170 leaders from across Asia and the world.

The map at the start of part B shows countries of Asia with Increase member bodies (dark shading) and other countries where some TEE work is also happening (light shading). Actually, Increase's definition of "Asia" is rather elastic. It includes the whole of the Middle East and spills slightly into North Africa; the Russian-speaking countries merge into Europe; and TEE follows the path of Asian diaspora all around the globe. Nevertheless, Asia remains the core focus of Increase's work.

Increase members unite around the same exciting vision: *Churches equipping all Christ's followers in their contexts, so that many millions are discipled and empowered for mission, ministry, and leadership.*

Increase's Activities

First, the Increase Association connects and strengthens church-based training movements across Asia. Its member organizations serve together to
- Build a network of good relationships
- Encourage collaborative projects and partnerships
- Initiate and catalyze innovative approaches
- Identify and share fruitful practice
- Provide support, resources, advice, and training.

Increase supports national teams, but it does not control them.

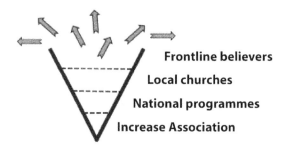

Individuals from Increase's member organizations give time to serve the wider membership. Some serve as Increase Equippers, giving a few days a year to travel and share their expertise with other programs. Others join a Task Group, coming together around a particular project that will benefit the whole Association. Some are on the Intercessors' Team, committed to pray regularly for the work of Increase. Some serve on Increase's Committee, currently chaired by Anneta Vysotskaya and previously by Richard Morris then Zafar Ismail. All of these voluntary contributions are coordinated by Increase's small serving base in Malaysia, with Tim Green as the General Secretary.

Second, as well as serving its own members, Increase makes a wider contribution. It seeks to

- Make a global contribution to theological education and adult learning
- Connect with other church-based training associations and accrediting associations
- Communicate widely the news and stories from Increase members.

Increase is an associate member of the Asia Theological Association (ATA) and contributes to its academic policy making and accreditation visits. Increase also leads workshops in the main conferences of ATA and the International Council for Evangelical Theological Education (ICETE) and takes part in discussions at the interface of residential and church-based training.

At the academic level, Increase seeks to take forward research and publication on TEE and other forms of church-based training. The bibliography in this book shows that recent writing is quite active even if not widely distributed. At the popular level, Increase publishes stories, including the ones in this book, to tell the news of what is happening through TEE in Asia today.

Looking to the Future

In today's changing world, TEE needs to look ahead, not backwards. It needs to keep adapting to be fit to fulfill its purpose in the twenty-first century. Increase seeks to foster innovation in TEE. "Increase is contributing creatively and effectively," says Dr Riad Kassis, former Director of ICETE.[1] Dr Marvin

---

1. From an email to Graham Aylett, 19 July 2013.

Oxenham of the ICETE Academy and the European Evangelical Accrediting Association believes that "TEE is clearly not a thing of the past, but one of the most exciting delivery innovations that calls our attention today."[2]

Increase's 2015 consultation, "Exploring New Horizons," established task groups to work on key areas for innovation and best practice in TEE. They continued their work in 2016 at "Moving Forward Together" and are now delivering results, while further areas have opened up more recently. Increase and its member movements are asking questions like these:

- How can TEE group leaders receive excellent training and support for their key role?
- How can new, transformative TEE courses be developed for twenty-first century Asia?
- How can the TEE movement harness the potential of digital technology?
- How can training organizations work together for integrated learning pathways?
- How can church-based training and residential training build good partnerships?
- How can TEE expand the reach of diaspora and be extended worldwide?

The next six chapters show how Increase is making progress in these areas or catalyzing it in partnership with others.

---

2. Dr Marvin Oxenham on his Facebook post, 29 June 2018, https://www.facebook.com/profile.php?id=100014831497159.

29

Equipping and Supporting
TEE Group Leaders

Graham Aylett

TEE learners are busy adults who have many claims on their time! They are unlikely to continue in a program unless they find it accessible, applicable, and affordable. Group meetings need to be engaging, enjoyable, and effective, helping members to grow together in a supportive group environment. In all of this program, the role of the group leader is key. What an important role the group leader has in the whole TEE methodology!

Good group leaders are vital for effective and fruitful TEE. So TEE programs and churches running groups must take care and prayer to find, train, encourage, and support their group leaders. TEE programs understand this, and it is appropriate that the Increase Association has given close attention to sharing and building on the experience that members have in training and supporting group leaders. Here are some of the milestones along the way.

2010: Twenty-First Century TEE in Asia – Challenges and Opportunities

At this conference, TEE programs pooled their experience and together created an outline for an effective training for new group leaders of SEAN's foundation course Abundant Life.[1] Two decisions were made: first, that trainees need to experience a good model of group discussion, and second, that trainees benefit from two opportunities to have a go at leading group discussion themselves. The first time around, inexperienced group leaders make all kinds of mistakes and may even dominate the discussion. But with a second chance, they have an opportunity to learn from those mistakes! Teams also began to identify core information – things that every TEE group leader should know, for instance a basic understanding of TEE methodology: personal study – group meeting – practical.

But how can trainers best deliver this core information? As group discussion is such an important part of the TEE method, a series of lectures is not the most appropriate way. Indeed, one of the challenges in many Asian contexts can be for group leaders to grasp that their role is not to lecture but to involve members in group discussion! Jane Vella's book *Taking Learning to Task* provided a really helpful answer.[2] Learning tasks provide a way for new group leaders to gain the knowledge they need in an interactive and effective way.

Late 2014 to 2015: Principles for Group Leader Training

After the initial steps in 2010, it became clear that partnership between TEE users would benefit from clearer training directions. When one program wants to use courses from another program, it is very helpful if they share an agreed baseline for acceptable training. In view of this, a joint SEAN/ Increase working group prepared guidelines for training new group leaders. They were produced in relation to training first-time users of SEAN's foundation course Abundant Life and were structured around eight principles:

1. Prepare the ground with a new user before setting up Group Leader Training.
2. Choose and prepare group leader trainers and coaches with great care.
3. Help a new user church or organization to make good choices of new group leaders.

---

1. SEAN, pronounced "say-an," stands for Study by Extension for All Nations (see chapter 5).
2. Jane Vella, *Taking Learning to Task: Creative Strategies for Teaching Adults* (San Francisco: Jossey-Bass, 2001).

4. Provide training that equips new group leaders to start leading a TEE group effectively.
5. Structure group leader training around group meetings.
6. Give all participants an opportunity to lead at least two group meetings with feedback.
7. Use teaching and learning methods that support the teaching and learning methods of a TEE group meeting.
8. Assess participants by providing an opportunity for them to demonstrate the knowledge, skills, and attitudes needed to lead a group.[3]

2015: Exploring New Horizons

Training and supporting group leaders was one of the key issues at this Increase conference, and a Task Group was formed to further explore group leader training. The eight principles were introduced and well received. Further thought was given to the qualities, knowledge, skills, and attitudes that new group leaders need and how they can be nurtured in effective training. You can read all about this conference in Training Group Leaders Effectively inserted after this chapter. TEE programs were encouraged to evaluate their own group leader training practice in the light of the principles.

2016: Moving Forward Together

Some of the members of the Task Group met together at this Increase conference. Each member of the Association serves in a particular country context, and different members of the Association have different curricula on different educational levels. The Task Group worked to identify group leader training packages that were good examples of the guidelines and principles applied in a range of contexts.

---

3. "Principles for TEE Group Leader Training," Increase Association, https://www.increaseassociation.org/resources/group-leader-training/67-principles-for-tee-group-leader-training.

2017: An Online Resource to Support on the Ground Group Leader Training

In response to a new start-up context in Malaysia, the Increase support team redesigned the group leader's manual for Abundant Life. This revision provided the key to running an effective one day group leader training which has been used to launch new groups among diaspora. On the basis of that experience, SEAN and Increase have collaborated with Khalibre, a provider of online training, to create an online training resource called Launching Effective Discipleship Groups Using TEE.[4]

Now it is possible for a group of people to receive initial training in TEE wherever they are in the world, even where a face-to-face workshop is impossible. People can start using TEE even where there is no national TEE program, or where workshops are few and far between, and also in the diaspora. This is a significant breakthrough which deserves celebrating! Just as TEE brought learning to people's doorsteps instead of having to relocate to a seminary, so this resource brings group leader training to the doorstep instead of having to travel to or wait for a workshop.

Once group leaders are actively leading groups, it does not mean their training is over. TEE programs have the continuing task of equipping group leaders with further knowledge and competence. And as volunteers, group leaders need recognition, encouragement, and prayer. Many TEE programs have found creative and fun ways to meet these needs.

At the end of this chapter, we pause to praise God and recognize the group leaders of the TEE movement. Perhaps you are one of them? We thank the Lord for your ministry! Our prayer is that, as well as the hard work of preparing for and leading groups, you will know great joy in seeing your group members grow and flourish as disciples of Jesus and in knowing that you are part of the fulfillment of Jesus's Great Commission.

May the Lord raise up many, many more who will commit to this ministry!

---

4. https://www.missiontools.org/resources/launching-effective-discipleship-groups-using-tee/. Contact increaseassociation@gmail.com for more details.

TRAINING GROUP LEADERS EFFECTIVELY

**Some Suggested Principles for TEE Group Leader Training
(Developed by SEAN International in 2015)**

TEE group leaders are prepared effectively in different ways in different programs. These principles have in mind a situation where a new user church or organization wants to start using TEE materials, and a national or regional TEE team visits the new user and runs a training workshop to prepare the first group leaders in that new situation.

1. Prepare the ground with new user *before* setting up group leader training. TEE programs are most fruitful with a good partnership between the program and the local user. The TEE program needs to understand the vision and context of the local user, and the local user needs to understand how to use TEE courses effectively and fruitfully.

2. Choose and prepare group leader trainers and coaches with great care. The experience, wisdom, knowledge, and attitudes of trainers who run the training and of any experienced group leaders who act as coaches during the training directly affect the quality of the training. A TEE program should choose and prepare trainers and coaches with great care.

3. Help the new user church or organization to make good choices of new group leaders. The choice of new group leaders, especially the very first group leaders, is very important for the future fruitfulness of the new TEE group, so it deserves prayer and great care. The TEE program's role is to make sure that the new user understands the general qualities of an effective and fruitful group leader.

4. Provide training that equips new group leaders to start leading a TEE group effectively. There is a core of knowledge, skills, and attitudes that

new group leaders need. By the end of group leader training, successful participants should demonstrate knowledge of the following:

- Some of the key Scriptures that nurture a passion for building up God's people through TEE, for example Matthew 28:18–20; Ephesians 4; and 2 Timothy 2:2, but others as well
- The three stages of TEE methodology: home study, group meetings, and practical application
- The use of the Group Leader's Guide
- The steps a group leader should take to prepare for each week's group meeting
- The characteristics of a good discussion
- The criteria for self-evaluation after a group discussion
- The qualities of an effective and fruitful group leader
- The requirements for successful course completion
- The reasons for assessment in adult learning

Successful participants should demonstrate competence to do the following:

- Use the Group Leader's Guide to prepare a lesson plan
- Lead a group meeting effectively, including
  - use the group meeting time effectively
  - listen well
  - ask good questions
  - involve all group members as appropriate
  - achieve the lesson objectives
- Help the group find and commit to appropriate practical application
- Evaluate themselves after they have led a group meeting
- Manage any tests or forms required for successful course completion

And by the end of the training, successful participants should show some signs of passion for the way God can build up his people using TEE.

5. Structure group leader training around group meetings. Giving a demonstration of key skills, opportunities for practice, and feedback is an effective way to structure group leader training.

- The skills involved in group leadership, like all skills, are learned through practice. So the training needs to provide opportunities to practice.
- Learning is most effective (and enjoyable!) when people are engaged and actively involved. Participants will learn best about group leadership when they are actively engaged in a group themselves.
- The experience of studying, exploring, and applying God's word together with others using TEE materials often gives participants a vision and a passion to use them.

6. Give all participants an opportunity to lead at least two group meetings with feedback. Although they should have just seen a demonstration of a good group meeting, many participants still give mini-sermons or lectures during the first group meeting they lead during training. So the feedback they receive can be discouraging! But leading a second group meeting gives them another chance to demonstrate that they are able to lead a group meeting effectively. Coaches and trainers are also able to assess them fairly and encourage them.

7. Use teaching and learning methods that support the teaching and learning methods of a TEE group meeting. Many people assume that lecturing is the most effective way to teach. If TEE group leaders understand themselves to be lecturing teachers, discussion in group meetings will be very limited! So group leader training based around lectures may reinforce the assumption that lecturing is the most effective way to teach. Therefore, group leader training should model a teaching and learning method that involves questions, discussion, and feedback. Learning tasks are also a powerful tool to help here.

8. Assess participants by providing an opportunity for them to demonstrate the knowledge, skills, and attitudes needed to lead a group. A simple test for core knowledge, observation of practicing group leadership core skills, and a simple question or a brief interview to determine attitudes will give participants an opportunity to show what they know, what they can do, and what their vision and passion is for using TEE materials.

30

Creating Twenty-First Century TEE Courses

Tim Green

Why New Courses?

Some TEE courses written in the 1970s and 1980s have stood the test of time, but others need significant revision. Most national TEE organizations have translated and adapted courses from outside their country. Only a few have written their own courses for their own contexts, and there is a real need to raise up a new generation of writers to develop new courses.

New courses are needed for at least five reasons. First because TEE curricula were originally developed to train pastors for church ministries, yet most TEE students today are lay people who need to be equipped to impact society, not just the church. New courses are needed to help them be salt and light, relevant witnesses, and able to serve their communities.

Second, Asian societies have changed much in recent decades. The 2015 Increase consultation "Exploring New Horizons" prioritized urgent issues in Asia today such as corruption and social injustice, marriage and family life, suffering and persecution, addictions, pornography, migrant workers, overpopulation, the environment, and children at risk. TEE courses do not yet exist on most of these topics. Today's Christians should be equipped for today's challenges.

Third, many Asian Christians are first-generation believers. Their upbringing in a non-Christian environment has shaped their mind-set, so deep-level discipleship is needed to help them form a new mind in Christ while still staying connected with their culture. This situation requires new discipleship courses that tackle specific worldview issues. The course *Come Follow Me* for Christ's followers of Muslim background aims at these issues, and other courses are being developed for Buddhist-background believers who have been influenced by animism.

Fourth, the digital age has quickly swept across Asia which has profound implications for TEE, as we will explore in chapter 31. Advanced technology creates opportunities for digital enrichment of existing courses and for bold new experiments in designing TEE study materials for the smartphone.

Finally, it is time for TEE course designers to look critically at existing materials and to benefit from the insights of educationalists on how adults learn well. New courses should bring *transformation*, not merely *information*. They may use a mix of innovative approaches to build on the proven TEE methodology and enhance it at the same time. As part B of this book has shown, transformation does already happen through TEE as God's Spirit applies the teaching to learners' lives. But course design could more intentionally help learners reflect on experience and connect truth with life. Moreover the Leaders' Guides could suggest a greater variety of learning activities in the group meetings and more accountable ways to check if the previous week's practical task has been fulfilled.

Increase's Training Scheme

Following the 2015 consultation, Increase established Task Groups to move forward in key areas. Two of these Task Groups, Training for Transformation and New Courses for Asia, worked together in 2016 to create a training scheme for course writers. Experience shows that a single workshop is insufficient to launch a new writer. To develop a TEE course from concept to completion is a marathon requiring much perseverance. Addressing this need, Increase's innovative scheme to train course writers is the first in Asia to offer a connected training over eighteen months supported by a mentor. It is a training pathway that supports authors in writing transformative courses for their specific context.

Aims of the Courses:

These new or revised TEE courses will help learners in community do the following:
- Shine the light of the Bible on specific situations in local contexts
- Integrate action and reflection intentionally
- Grow more Christ-like in knowledge, attitudes, abilities, and relationships
- Be transformed themselves and to help bring transformation in their circles of influence.[1]

The Topics

Eleven writing teams from ten national TEE programs were formed, with SEAN International sending one more team. The writers were carefully selected by their national directors, and together they chose which courses to develop, prioritizing topics that excited the writers and would help to fill curriculum gaps. The writers could tackle other topics later after gaining skills and confidence in producing courses themselves.

Most teams chose to create brand new courses, while others undertook major adaptations of existing courses to bring them into today's context. Several teams chose similar topics but were encouraged to develop these in their own way for their own contexts. The topics include the following:
- Pre-marriage relationships
- Marriage and family life (three independent teams in different contexts)
- Parenting the second generation
- Discipleship challenges for believers of Muslim background
- Youth ministry
- Spirit world and folk religion
- Spirit world (revision)

---

1. This definition evolved through different versions and was finalized at the Course Writers Workshop in Mongolia, 20–23 March 2017.

- Spiritual disciplines (adapted for e-learners)
- Responses to persecution and suffering
- Responding well to persecution (two teams)

The First Writing Stage

Increase devised a sequence of three writing stages over eighteen months. The first stage of the process started in March 2017 with a workshop followed by a research phase. In the workshop, writers learned that *understanding their context* must come before *writing the content*. So this initial workshop equipped participants to research the answers to the following questions:

- What is the current situation in their context?
- What would a transformed situation look like in the light of God's word?
- How can the planned course aim to change learners so that they start to change their situations?

Following the workshop, the trainee writers conducted interviews and surveys to find out the needs in their particular context. One in Mongolia contacted no less than 192 people!

The Second Writing Stage

Starting in June 2017, this stage enabled participants to practise writing skills and to start work on their first drafts. They used their research findings to work out what the course objectives should be, and from there created an outline and draft chapter. Newly written chapters came to life and were tested immediately in small groups, and bonds of friendship developed within the cohort of trainees as they faced the same challenges together. The workshop was followed by a year of writing to develop course content, the learning tasks, and the Leaders' Guide. All of the teams made some progress, but some struggled. However, six teams had all or most of their course written after a year. Throughout this period, writers connected with their mentors over email or Skype.

The Third Writing Stage

The last stage began in June 2018 with a workshop to teach the skills required to get the course ready for publication. Participants were equipped in the areas of assessment, field testing, writing group Leaders' Guides, and formatting. This stage will be completed when each team has printed and launched their new course.

Benefitting from Educational Expertise

An important feature of this training scheme was the excellent group of mentors who came together to run it. Some like Dr Patricia Harrison, Dr Allan Harkness, and Dr Perry Shaw are widely recognized for their educational expertise. Dr Tim Green and Freda Carey also have much experience in TEE course development. Perspectives in digital and blended learning were brought by Dr Rosemary Dewerse and Rev David Burke and in experiential learning by Nicholas Ivins. This shared expertise enriched the program and will help connect it to wider theological education. As the current cohort of writers hopes to complete their courses, further steps are on the horizon. One of them is to improve the training package and put parts of it online. Another is to offer the training more widely to raise up more course writers who will tackle the challenges that Asian Christians face today.

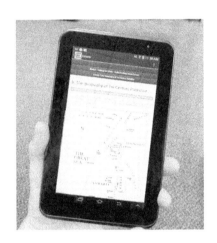

**Personal study for TEE courses
now possible on a mobile phone**

31

Exploring Digital Opportunities

Tim Green

We live in a digital age. New technologies offer creative new ways to access information, connect people, and give space for them to work together. "Digital" has advantages over "paper" in several areas: many people prefer it, storage can be more secure in areas of persecution, and materials can be accessed globally. Online resources and training materials are available in many languages.

So is the TEE movement getting left behind? Is it still presenting and delivering courses in an old fashioned way? There is a risk that it is. The Increase Association is aware of this challenge and has made some progress, but much remains to be done. We move forward by learning from the steps already being taken by our member organizations, combined with advice from external consultants in digital learning.

Initiatives from National TEE Organizations

The country of Nepal might not be perceived as a hub of digital innovation. Yet its TEE movement ITEEN has pioneered initiatives in this area due to their Director Tanka Subedi and another team member called ND Lama who are both Increase Equippers. Through Facebook they communicate with their TEE group leaders even in remote parts of the country, and by the same means they receive student attendance records and exam scripts. They created a Moodle version of the Abundant Life course and a different smartphone version combining script and audio for slow readers. ND Lama is currently trying an experimental way to lead group meetings through Skype discussion, backed up by WhatsApp group contact.

Moreover, ITEEN was the first TEE program in Asia to use an online print-on-demand supplier. This does not mean the courses are studied online, but that they can be ordered online for local printing. For instance when course books are required for the Nepali diaspora in the West, they no longer need to be shipped or carried from Nepal. The TEE group leader simply orders and pays online, then the online supplier promptly prints and dispatches the books though the local mail. The TEE diaspora group no longer has to wait for courses to be sent from the motherland, and the national TEE program is saved much nuisance and expense. Also it is easy to produce a revised version because there is no old stock to use up. As diaspora TEE spreads worldwide in different languages, print on demand will be increasingly needed whether through online or local printers.

E-learning

Another Increase Association member is the Program for Theological Education by Extension (PTEE) serving the Arab world. Its e-learning stream was conceived back in 2008 and is led by Dr Rick Weymouth. His colleague Shereen Karadsheh is writing several courses directly in Arabic. Working at the interface of TEE and e-learning, she has been introduced through Increase to the expertise of mentors like Dr Rosemary Dewerse. In turn, Increase benefits from PTEE's innovative work at this frontier.

Rick Weymouth has taught at Increase workshops and developed thoughtful guidelines in "Issues to Consider as You Move Forward in E-learning."[1] He believes that in TEE, "e-learning should be used to enhance what is already being

---

1. Rick Weymouth, "E-Learning and TEE," paper presented to workshop participants at the Increase conference in Chiang Mai, 13–17 November 2017. Compiled of four short papers. This document contains "E-Learning and TEE: An Introductory Paper," 2010; "Issues to Consider as You Move Forward in E-Learning," 2010; "Issues to Consider as You Move Forward in E-Learning," 2017; "Relationality in E-Learning for PTEE," 2009.

done, rather than to replace it. For example, to remove the weekly face-to-face group seminar from TEE would mean eliminating an essential component of that which constitutes TEE."[2] However, a blended approach of face-to-face and online group interaction can combine the best of both, he believes. Also the step-by-step design of TEE lessons means that "relatively very little work is needed to convert a TEE course into an effective electronic course."[3] As an Increase Equipper, Rick helps its member organizations better understand e-learning. He also makes a wider contribution through the Asia Theological Association and the International Council for Evangelical Theological Education (ICETE). Increase members writing courses about TEE for the ICETE academy will gain further experience in e-learning. Partnership is yielding dividends.

Servant Not Master

Despite the great potential of e-learning, Rick and other educationalists also warn about its limitations. They agree that technology should remain the servant of education, not its master. When technology takes control, the learner is pushed into second place. To avoid this danger while moving ahead with e-learning opportunities, Increase teamed up with two other organizations: SEAN International contributed its courses while technological expertise came from MAF Learning Technologies, later called Edutech.

Together we asked some fundamental questions about good design for adult learning. Which parts of the four educational domains of knowing, doing, being, and relating (see chapter 4) can be mirrored in an online environment and which cannot? Purely online courses can be effective for knowing domain, though with the risk of displacing the other domains or ignoring the learner's local context. The doing domain likewise requires a local setting with local accountability. The being and relating domains can partially be developed through online reflection and chat rooms. Nevertheless in most Asian cultures, people still prefer to communicate orally in a real place and drinking real tea together.

TEE's group-based learning would lose its soul if it were transferred totally to a setting where individuals merely sit at their computer screen. However,

---

2. Weymouth, "E-Learning and TEE," 3.
3. Weymouth, 7.

there are many opportunities for digital technology to enrich the traditional TEE method rather than replace it. One example is inserting web links in course materials to enable students to access new information. Or group meetings may happen by Skype on occasion, and members can keep connected through social media to share prayer requests with each other. Their leader can give guidance and receive assignments in the same way. Thus digital technology is welcome, so long as it remains a servant and does not become master of the learning process.

A Blended Way to Train TEE Group Leaders

In 2017, members of Increase and SEAN tried something new. Until then a training workshop for new group leaders could only take place when a facilitator could come in and lead it. An online seminar might be a good way to overcome this problem, but it doesn't fit with the training. After all, leading a group is something that can only be learned in practice and with immediate feedback. So how could this practical workshop be blended with technology?

As explained in chapter 29, an answer came in the form of an online resource which can be downloaded anywhere in the world by a group of four or five people who are ready to be trained. The workshop facilitator is replaced by online guidance and clips. But the face-to-face group is still needed so participants can take turns leading discussion and getting feedback from each other. Thus this new training resource uses a blended approach to open up new horizons for training group leaders. It is an example of how technology can be the servant but not the master of education.

The Smartphone Revolution

Back in 2006 when Increase began, it was a puzzle to know how to put course materials into a digital format without excluding most learners in Asia. At that time few Asians owned their own computer, and fewer still had reliable internet. Even today online access is still limited for some by budget, internet availability, or the monitoring of suspicious governments.

But then came the smartphone. Once its price tumbled and it was supported by good mobile networks, this astonishing device swept across

Asia like a tsunami. Smartphone ownership spread from wealthy tycoons to street sweepers in just a few short years. Yesterday when I was on a Singapore commuter train, every single one of the travelers opposite me was heads-down on their phones. "Well," you may reply, "that's Singapore!" But in Bangladesh, peasant farmers check the rice price on their smartphones, and security guards watch films on theirs at night. These two examples are real proof that the smartphone has penetrated Asia.

Suddenly it has become possible for national TEE movements to overcome the earlier obstacles. No longer can only a few TEE students get online. Most can now do so through a device they already have in their pockets. No longer is online interaction restricted to written threads on Moodle, for now they can use Skype or WhatsApp for audio or visual conversations. No longer do they need to leave their device at home when attending group meetings, for now it is sitting in their palm.

This scenario is still futuristic in some Asian countries, but it won't stay that way for long. So the Increase Association is working with technology partners to see how to make TEE lessons usable on phones and tablets. We had high hopes that the first pilot app could be used in a country where persecuted Christians face a heavy fine if they are caught with a TEE book in their hand. But we found that the underlying software platforms kept shifting too fast. Now a new effort is beginning that uses a webapp approach which should hopefully avoid those problems.

Moving Forward

Despite setbacks, we cannot abandon the quest. The simple step-by-step design of TEE lessons naturally suits adaptation to a small screen, and pictures can be inserted, too. Then the material can be further enriched by adding links to video clips that students can view privately or in the group. Smartphones and tablets are the way forward in Asia, not computers.

Members of the Increase Association are helping each other to move forward in the digital age. But progress has been modest till now, while the technology leaps forward at a dizzying speed. Younger people are adapting to it faster than are TEE course designers. So adapting to the digital age remains an urgent challenge if twenty-first century TEE is to remain relevant.

**Nepali group leaders being thanked for their hard
work at a conference in Malaysia**
© ML Low. Used with permission.

32

Integrated Learning Pathways

Tim Green

In chapter 19 on Pakistan, we told the story of Rashid, a man who never went to school. But taking TEE courses at the Open Theological Seminary (OTS) gave him the opportunity to complete thirty courses all the way up to the degree level. This learning took him many years! But all this time he was using what he learned, becoming a pastor and serving God even while he continued on his own learning pathway. This way of learning worked for Rashid because OTS created enough courses in a graded progression to enable him to follow a connected pathway. But this is not the case in all TEE programs. So the Increase Association is raising the following questions in the community of theological educators.

A Theological Question about the Ministry of All Believers

The Reformation brought out the priesthood of all believers but not necessarily the ministry of all believers. There has been a tendency to treat ministers and members or laity as two different species: one to lead, the other to be led. The first group are equipped with "theological education"; the second group passively receive "Christian education." No matter how many Christian education courses a person completes, they do not at all qualify as the person's theological education.

But why this glass ceiling? Is it theologically valid? The vision for every TEE member ministry requires equipping every member. Not all church members will become leaders like Rashid, but the pathways should be available for some to evolve into leadership according to their calling and character.

An Educational Question about Designing Intentional Pathways

Chapter 4 explained a process of course design which starts with the learner in their context and leads to appropriate objectives and course design. But learners don't stay static. They change over time. Over the course of many years of TEE study, Rashid developed in personal maturity as he grew older, in academic ability because the earlier courses enabled him to cope with the harder ones, and in ministry because he was growing as a pastor. Rashid's movement can be visualized on the chart:

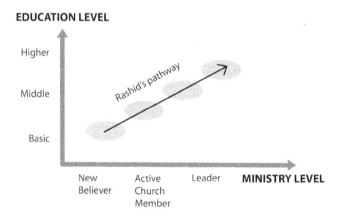

Designing courses for Rashid would follow the same process as in chapter 4 but applied to a moving target. Thus Rashid did not need thirty courses all at the same level but a progression of courses to keep stretching him on the learning pathway.

An Institutional Question about Building Synergy

There is a growing trend to bring in free-floating, short modules on individual topics from outside Asia and teach them as "intensives." Sometimes these modules are joined into curricula, but more often they are one-time events. A person can go from one short training to another collecting certificates, but where does it lead? One mission leader, perhaps unkindly, calls this a "dump and depart" model.[1]

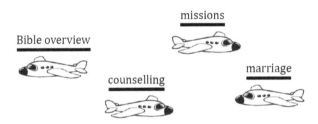

But there is value in these training events. Often they have been developed and refined by experts in their field who have many resources at their disposal. Yet these trainings are not locally rooted. By contrast, the TEE organizations in Asia are rooted in their context, like a ladder firmly anchored in the ground. They in turn lack resources and subject expertise. And few of them can provide a complete ladder like OTS. Mostly they focus on the lower and middle levels and have some missing rungs.

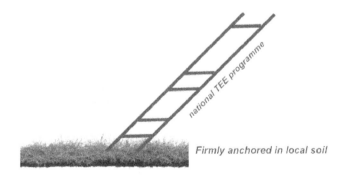

Firmly anchored in local soil

---

1. Personal communication to the authors, January 2018.

So could training institutions come together and create synergy? Could external courses created by specialists provide the missing rungs, linking in with the locally rooted TEE organizations for the benefit of both? Could they pool their efforts to construct a connected training ladder with rungs supplied by different providers but the uprights anchored in local soil and accountable to the churches?

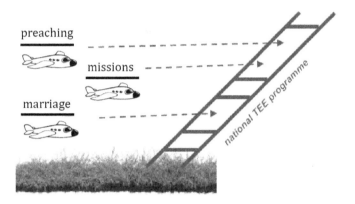

A Question of Accreditation

Our current accreditation systems favor the higher rungs. "They give no attention to the lower rungs; they say 'that's not our concern,'" commented one TEE leader.[2] Accordingly, the lower rungs may be discounted altogether or be forced to shift further up the ladder by adding extra academic requirements, even if these don't serve the learners.

Of course there is a valid place for academic assessment. But it tends to copy a university model where the mind is all that matters. In Christian ministry, it is just as important to evaluate skills, character, and relationships. Thankfully the Asia Theological Association (ATA) is concerned for balanced assessment in all these areas. Currently it accredits six of Increase's member organizations, while three Increase Equippers serve on the ATA's Commission

---

2. Rev Dr Qaiser Julius at the TEE Equippers forum, Bangkok, 13–16 June 2011.

for Accreditation and Educational Development, which provides a good forum to discuss appropriate accreditation for TEE.

In such circles, Increase is asking how accreditation should work for those TEE programs which provide a connected pathway from a basic foundation level all the way up to degree level. Also, what kind of quality assurance can work for non-formal theological education? These questions are under healthy discussion.

It may help to think first about fitness *of* purpose: Is each rung designed appropriately for its own place in the ladder? Second, we should think about fitness *for* purpose: Does the training at that level actually fulfill its designed intent? All rungs need to be strong enough to support the learner at that level. A lower level rung can be just as strong as a higher rung, so long as it works well at its own place in the ladder. For example, does the training equip a Hindu-background believer to stand firm in Christ, or a businessperson to work and witness with integrity, or a bi-vocational church planter to start a new congregation, or a pastor to lead a large church, or a scholar to write a commentary? In each case, the training needs to fulfill its own designed purpose.

Looking to the Future

Much in this chapter is speculative. As yet we have few examples to show in practice, though the learning ladders are gradually being extended in countries like Bangladesh, South Korea, Nepal, and Russia. But the Increase Association looks to a future where many more people like Rashid can be helped to flourish through integrated pathways. Hopefully in the next five years, we will see more progress.

TEE group leaders from across Mongolia sharing at a
training session organized by Mongolia TEE

33

Partnership with Residential Institutions

Graham Aylett and Hanna-Ruth van Wingerden

Increase members are serving the churches in their contexts with tools to equip and empower their church members. Most residential institutions aim to prepare pastors and leaders for local churches. There is great potential here for synergy as residential institutions put the tools of TEE into the hands and hearts of their students so that they are better equipped to equip their future congregations!

Although this is the most obvious possibility for partnership, it is not the only possibility. At the 2016 Asia Theological Association General Assembly, Increase presented a number of different areas for mutually beneficial partnership between church-based and residential programs with examples from around Asia. Some of these areas for partnership are presented here.

Area A: Prior Church-Based TEE Prepares Students for More Fruitful Residential Training

Some residential seminaries face the challenge of falling enrolment and are searching for ways to encourage more people to study. They may also face pressure to lower their entry requirements. Yet "The Cape Town Commitment" of the Lausanne Movement affirms the need for careful selection: "Biblically, only those whose lives already display basic qualities of mature discipleship should be appointed to leadership."[1]

Meanwhile in many countries, TEE programs only offer courses up to the certificate or at most the diploma level. It takes time and resources to develop higher-level courses, and the students themselves may not want to spend many years completing their part time degrees! Some may want to complete their studies and are attracted by the community life and library facilities offered by seminaries.

So one way of building a win-win partnership is for learners to be equipped in their own churches through TEE learning groups in preparation for residential study. They may even study until they have completed a certificate program, potentially the equivalent of the first year of residential training. Equipping believers through church-based TEE can also create a larger pool from which seminary students may grow. Even better, the commitment of these students will have been tested. They will also have developed good study habits and proved themselves in ministry in their local churches. They may well be more mature and have a much richer life experience. From this pool, good students could transfer to the second year of a three-year program at seminary.

The College of Christian Theology Bangladesh (CCTB) goes one step further. They offer a BTh program in three stages. The first two stages are delivered through church-based training in local learning groups throughout Bangladesh. These first two stages may take ten or more years to complete. The third stage is taught residentially at the CCTB campus in Dhaka for one year. The completed training combines the advantages of TEE and residential education.

Area B: TEE Courses as Part of the Seminary Curriculum

There are different ways that TEE courses can be used in a seminary curriculum, and we will introduce a few examples that show how this kind of partnership can benefit seminaries, students, TEE programs, and churches.

---

1. "The Cape Town Commitment," IID, 3, Christ-centered leaders, Lausanne Movement, October 2010, https://www.lausanne.org/content/ctcommitment.

TEE Courses Enriching the Curriculum

In Pakistan, some residential institutes use TEE courses to enrich their curriculum. TEE courses are prepared by subject experts who are part of a team, and the resulting courses enable the seminary to offer classes on topics for which they may not have the appropriate faculty. The Open Theological Seminary (OTS) Director Dr Qaiser Julius comments on the benefits for OTS and seminaries:

> On both sides, I think it is very beneficial. The residential institutions are able to use OTS courses when they don't have a lecturer or the expertise to teach a subject. They could use OTS courses with a group leader. The residential institution does not have to prepare the whole course, which is a demanding task.[2]

TEE Courses Integrated into the Curriculum

Other seminaries in Pakistan have made TEE courses an integral part of the curriculum. Zarephath Bible Seminary made TEE part of their three-year BTh course: students do at least six TEE courses. And as they experience small group dynamics, they gain a real appreciation for the methodology. (Read more about this partnership in chapter 19.)

The Presbyterian seminary in Vladivostok, Russia gives students the opportunity to take TEE courses from ORTA. (Read more about ORTA in chapter 26.) Lee Young Hoon, Principal from 2010 to 2014, evaluated the benefits he observed, "The ORTA program trains seminary students for ministry in local churches, makes for personal spiritual growth of ministers, and develops qualities needed to communicate with people. The ORTA program is very helpful for residential theological institutions."[3]

TEE Group Leader Training Integrated into the Curriculum

The seminary in Vladivostok also trains every student as an ORTA group leader so that when they graduate, they are equipped with this tool for ministry. Another example of using TEE for group leader training is in a Central Asian

---

2. Dr Qaiser Julius to Graham Aylett, Skype interview, July 2016.
3. Lee Young Hoon, in personal communication to ORTA staff members.

seminary. This seminary knows the need for appropriate systematic theology and the knowledge base needed for ministry. But they also see the need for practical tools that students can use when they become church planters or full-time ministers. The Academic Director shared,

> When I started using SEAN materials in my church, I saw good results. I witnessed people change and grow. The Lord gave me the idea to include Abundant Life, Abundant Light, and The Life of Christ in the seminary curriculum. I am happy that we not only give the students knowledge but also equip them practically for their future ministry.[4]

Leading TEE Groups as a Fieldwork Placement

Because practical ministry is an essential part of ministry training, some seminaries include leadership of a TEE group in a local church as a fieldwork placement or practicum. Zarephath Bible Seminary gives third year BTh students this opportunity for their practical ministries. Once students graduate, they have proven competence, and have confidence, in leading a TEE group.

The Malaysia Baptist Theological Seminary (MBTS) works in partnership with TEE Movers for the Chinese Church (TMCC) using Chinese language courses. (Read more about TMCC in chapter 23.) The Associate Director for MBTS Lim Sai Mooi comments,

> I would like my students to study Bible courses in seminary which they can also teach in the church. The six books of The Life of Christ serve as a base for the other Bible and theology classes. We have a teachers' guide book that helps the local group leaders so our students can become teachers, too. In this way, more Christians will study The Life of Christ in different churches, and their life will change.[5]

---

4. Written testimony to Graham Aylett, sent via the International Director of ORTA.
5. Lim Sai Mooi, email to Graham Aylett, 20 July 2016.

Area C: Partnership for TEE Course Development

Seminaries can help develop TEE courses. With their expertise and access to resources, seminary faculty are well placed to play an important role in course-writing teams. This area of partnership has led to many new TEE courses across Asia and can be very beneficial as long as experts in TEE methodology are part of the course-writing team. There is a lot of work in transforming a professor's lectures into a good church-based training course!

Likewise, TEE programs can help seminaries to develop online courses. As residential schools move to online learning, they may draw on the principles and approaches of church-based training. For example, the Teach-Learn project in the Arab world adopted and adapted church-based training courses developed by the Program for Theological Education by Extension (PTEE) for use in their online program.

In Conclusion

What enormous benefits there could be to local churches all across Asia from mutual understanding and partnership between church-based and residential training institutions! If you are serving in residential theological education, equipping your students as future church leaders, and want to explore these possibilities with the Increase Association, please contact us at increaseassociation@gmail.com.

TEE knows no boundaries. A Nepali worker was discipled in Malaysia
and receives his TEE certificate from the ITEEN (Nepal) Director

34

Expanding the Reach
of Diaspora TEE

Tim Green

Globalization in the twenty-first century means that the phenomenon of "diaspora" Christian communities is becoming more and more important. About 250 million people live away from their country of birth. Some have moved away to study, some to work, some to escape. This diaspora, Greek for "scattering," is a major trend in the modern world, but it has not taken God by surprise. He is using the diaspora to bring people to him.

In part B of this book, we see how TEE is being used to equip groups of Christ's followers in diaspora. This chapter focusses on the particular contribution of Increase to help facilitate this process. Since 2014, this work has been taken forward by SEAN and Increase in close collaboration. Increase has a Task Group on diaspora TEE and five Equippers who have a special interest in this area.

Discipling the Diaspora

When host churches or Christian fellow migrants share God's love and migrants become believers, the task of discipleship follows. But how may these new believers – who speak different languages – be discipled and equipped?

TEE groups can be a solution since they allow people to grow as disciples in their mother tongue and enable some to become leaders of migrant fellowships.

But this discipleship requires multi-language materials to be readily available. SEAN courses are a flexible resource as they are already translated in eighty languages. Temporary migrants like to study in their heart language, as do first-generation settlers, but their children usually prefer to use the host country language. Thus bilingual provision is needed when TEE spans diaspora generations.

How Increase Is Helping

The Increase Association believes strongly that diaspora mission is God's call for this season. Therefore diaspora TEE was highlighted at the 2017 Increase conference "Empowering Churches, Equipping Disciples." At the conference close, participants declared the statement given at the end of this chapter which gave Increase a direction to pursue over the next five years.

Connecting People with Opportunities

Conference statements have their place, but more organic initiatives happen when people connect around a shared vision. One participant at the 2017 Increase conference was Dmitrii Hen, who pastors a Russian-speaking diaspora church in Korea. At the conference, he met the Russian and Central Asian TEE teams, saw their materials, and was inspired. He invited those TEE teams to come and lead training for his and other migrant churches. Just a month later, they came and ran two workshops which quickly led to several TEE groups being formed.

Similar spontaneous energy was released at the 2015 Increase gathering when Nepali TEE leaders met Malaysian Christians who were already seeking a systematic, biblical way to disciple Nepali migrant workers. In chapter 14, this encounter is described as a "divine appointment." Divine it was, but there was a human element, too. The Increase hosts intentionally placed those people together. It was just a case of being a catalyst for action to happen.

Advising on the Practicalities

A shared vision is the first step, but practical action is also needed to create a sustainable TEE program for the diaspora. This program is built on a partnership between two key parties: the TEE organization who created or translated the courses and the diaspora group in another country wanting to use them. When these two parties are connected, they have to agree on a realistic way to provide books or print them locally, a fair way to handle the finances, an effective way to train group leaders, and an efficient way to keep student records. Increase's contribution in these processes is to advise on how to make these practicalities happen and to help the two parties build trust.

Catalyzing Diaspora TEE in New Places

Increase Equippers with diaspora experience are seeking how best to catalyze new opportunities, which very much depends on God's leading. Just before this chapter was written, they were testing the potential for diaspora TEE in the Arabian Gulf. With so many Asian Christians working there, it seemed like an excellent opportunity. TEE leaders from Pakistan, India, Bangladesh, Jordan, Nepal, and the Philippines were ready to introduce TEE to migrant workers from their countries. Yet despite drawing up plans, the response did not materialize as expected.

While wondering what to do next, Increase received an invitation from Australia to run a TEE consultation in Sydney. Here a large cohort of Chinese Christian leaders had completed the six-part *Life of Christ* course and were ready to start their own TEE groups. Australia also offered opportunities with other diaspora groups and languages. So is God postponing the Gulf idea in order to redirect attention to Asians in Australia? The question is open at the time of writing this chapter, but this situation illustrates how Increase tries to follow God's lead.

Making the Case Globally for Diaspora TEE

The international Lausanne Movement has had a diaspora track for some time, but without seeing TEE as part of the picture. That began to change when one of their leaders, Dr Sadiri Joy, attended the Increase conference and was inspired. In turn two Increase Equippers, Rachel Green and Rosana Longgat, attended the Lausanne diaspora conference and presented the case for making TEE part of the picture of serving the diaspora worldwide, which is leading to further opportunities.

Conclusion

As diaspora and global migration patterns will continue to grow in importance, Increase strives to actively join in with what God is doing among Christians in Asia and beyond. Responding to Jesus's command to make disciples of all nations, Increase will keep looking for ways to help churches disciple the nations wherever they are scattered.

INCREASE CONFERENCE
DIASPORA STATEMENT

Prepared by Dr David Ball and the Diaspora Task Group. Declared by the "Empowering Churches, Equipping Disciples" conference participants in Chiang Mai, 17 November 2017[1]

Empowering Churches and Equipping Disciples in the Asian Diaspora

We recognise that people groups are migrating across our region of Asia and around the world more than ever before.

We see that God is building his church in a new and exciting way through these diaspora communities.

We share a common vision for training resources to be made available across Asia and beyond to equip all Christian believers to grow in Christ and serve him actively in their local churches and communities.

We commit to work together over the next five years to

- Actively support and encourage those with a vision to empower churches in discipling diaspora believers in Asia and beyond.
- Make discipleship and leadership resources available to those who wish to use them for group learning in local churches.
- Partner with like-minded churches, organizations, and networks in Asia and beyond to enable discipleship, ministry, and mission training to take place among and through diaspora believers.

---

1. https://www.increaseassociation.org/images/resources-library/diaspora-statement.pdf.

Increase Conference in Chiang Mai 2017
© ML Low. Used with permission.

35

TEE: Looking to the Future

Tim Green

This book gives abundant evidence that God continues to use TEE in many ways, in many lives, and in many countries across Asia. We have seen how new believers are being discipled, local leaders equipped in their context, persecuted Christians strengthened, the diaspora reached, and churches changed. This movement is still growing. Half a century after the birth of TEE, reports of its death are premature!

Still Relevant in the Twenty-First Century

The world church is looking for ways to equip all of God's people to fulfill his call to mission in his world. Two different streams of global Christianity made this same point in the same year. The International Study Group on Theological Education for the Edinburgh 2010 Congress stated that "Educating the whole people of God is a key to mission."[1] In the same year, the Lausanne Movement declared its conviction that "We need intensive efforts to train all God's people in whole-life discipleship, which means to live, think, work, and

---

1. Dietrich Werner and Namsoon Kang, "Theme 6 Theological Education and Formation," in *Mission Today and Tomorrow*, edited by Kirsteen Kim and Andrew Anderson (Regnum Books International, 2011), 160.

speak from a biblical worldview and with missional effectiveness in every place or circumstance of daily life and work."[2]

These are wonderful aspirations, but how will they be fulfilled in practice? TEE offers a proven route to help fulfill them on a global scale but in locally relevant ways. The Edinburgh working group believed that "Decentralized TEE programs for most of Christianity in the South will prove to be one of the most effective and most widely spread models of theological education in the twenty-first century."[3] And the Lausanne Movement Director Lindsay Brown stated, "TEE programs coordinated by experienced, culturally sensitive and theologically-aware trainers provide a substantial answer to this problem of grass-roots training of believers, in their context, for their context."[4]

Other theological educators agree. Dr Thomas Schirrmacher affirmed, "The World Evangelical Alliance sees TEE training as an integral part of the evangelical world . . . a much needed answer for theological training under persecution."[5] Dr Manfred Kohl says, "I am convinced that in the next generation . . . TEE will produce far more trained pastors for the church than the traditional institutions of the past."[6]

Explaining TEE in a Fresh Way

Despite the past impact of TEE and its continuing relevance today, it suffers from an image problem. Some mission leaders and theological educators have never heard of it, while others dismiss what they assume it to be. But the TEE movement itself has done a poor job of communication in recent decades. Its publications are not well known, and many national TEE programs have no website. Practitioners have not done enough to tell the stories of what is

---

2. "The Cape Town Commitment," Part IIA, 3.C, https://www.lausanne.org/content/ctcommitment#p2-1, accessed 3 September 2018.

3. Edinburgh International Study Group on Theological Education, *Challenges and Opportunities in Theological Education in the 21st Century: Pointers for a New International Debate on Theological Education* (Joint Information Service of ETE & WOCATI, 2009), 35.

4. Lindsay Brown, email to Tim Green.

5. Dr Thomas Schirrmacher stated at the Increase conference in Kathmandu, 4–8 October 2010.

6. Manfred Waldemar Kohl, "Theological Education: What Needs to Be Changed?" *Torch Trinity Journal* 12 (2009): 156.

happening or to engage with current trends in theological education. This book makes a start in changing that, but much more is needed.

The very label "TEE" needs to be explained to those who have never heard it, and re-explained to those who have. In Increase, we started to address this issue in 2011. We asked some experienced TEE leaders in Asia how they would explain its essence in a single phrase. Their responses included the following:[7]

- On-the-job discipleship training for all believers
- Leadership education on location
- Hands-on ministry training
- Local learning groups
- Open learning for Christian living
- Church-based leadership training
- Equipped to serve where you are
- Community learning for Christian ministry
- Ministry action learning

Then we asked the TEE leaders how they would describe TEE in a sentence They proposed the following:

- Through local learning groups, TEE gives people on-the-job training for Christian life and ministry.
- TEE equips God's people in their context for their context so that every believer becomes a disciple, and every disciple a worker for Jesus.
- TEE is a framework for training disciples, including leaders, which combines individual study, group discussion, and practical assignments in the local context.
- TEE empowers Christ's followers through local learning groups to serve him in church and society.
- TEE is a simple, locally owned, cost effective, situationally relevant, and holistic means of discipleship and equipping for Christian ministry at all levels.

Next, we asked the leaders if they would like to abandon altogether the label "TEE." Some Westerners present favored this idea because "Theological Education by Extension" is a cumbersome phrase that is not well understood

---

7. TEE Equippers at a consultation in Bangkok, 13–16 June 2010, in the meeting of 16 June 2010.

and not very accurate in describing TEE today. But the Asians made a firm response along these lines:

> You Westerners first gave us the term TEE, and you can't now tell us to drop it. We incorporated it into the names of our organizations. In India, people know what TAFTEE is and what it does. They don't know what the initials stand for, and they don't care. So it's your problem, not ours. We are happy with the term TEE.[8]

Their argument prevailed in Increase, which is an Asian association of Asian national organizations. So the name "TEE" is here to stay. However, we can explain it in a fresh way by using the same initials to mean Tools to Equip and Empower. It's not a perfect phrase, and it doesn't cover everything we want to say. But it certainly raises interest, unlike "Theological Education by Extension," which tends to close it down.

Needed Areas of Renewal

It's true that TEE needs a new image. But image is less important than substance. What is the substance of TEE? Is it really living up to its claims? Is it renewing itself in the twenty-first century? How can good practice spread from one country to another? What new horizons should be explored? Asia today is very different from the Asia of fifty years ago, so is TEE responding to the changes and challenges?

Linked and supported through the Increase Association, Asian TEE movements are gaining the capacity to start addressing these questions. The 2010 conference linked them across the continent. For most participants, this was their first opportunity to glimpse wider TEE horizons than in their own country. This conference created bonds of networked trust that led to the discovery of expertise among us and the release of energy for shared initiatives. It also created the self-confidence to be able to look critically at ourselves. Since then, as an Association of these national movements, Increase has been able to embark on specific areas of renewal and improvement.

---

8. Dr David Samuel and other TEE leaders in the TEE Equippers consultation in Bangkok, 13–16 June 2010.

Some of these areas are described in chapters 29–34. The TEE movement in Asia is seeking to strengthen weaker areas and explore new horizons. Since the training and support of TEE group leaders is often a weak link, we have learned from each other and developed better ways to do both. As most TEE courses are long established and translated from outside, Asian writers are now being trained to create new courses in their own languages for their own contexts and with a new attention to transformative learning. Responding to the rapid spread of digital technology, we are exploring ways to make the most of it while preserving good educational design. Seeking better synergy with formal and non-formal theological educators, we are opening up discussion about integrated learning pathways and institutional partnerships. Believing that mission is seeing what God is doing and joining in, we see God working among globally scattered peoples and want to play our part in discipling the diaspora.

Work is already underway in all of these areas and is just starting on good governance, creative communications, and sustainable funding. So there is much to be done. In all of these areas, Increase can share good ideas and offer advice among its members. But it will not control them, for they are self-governing entities who make their own decisions. Progress will be faster in some places than in others, especially as most TEE national programs are limited by financial and human resources.

For the TEE movement to be well tuned to the future, it needs to learn from the past and the present. This learning requires more than merely collecting the stories of impact, inspiring though they are. Objective field research is also needed. One example is the doctoral research carried out by Dr Stephen Cho, who investigated the retention rate for Korean students from one TEE course to the next. This honest self-examination helped TEE Korea adjust its curriculum so that a greater proportion of students continued. Some examples of field research are mentioned in the bibliography. But much more remains to be done.

Looking beyond TEE itself, the Increase Association would like to connect more with other types of church-based training in Asia and the Middle East. Learning from these other approaches will help bring renewal in the TEE movement, and hopefully the benefit will be mutual. Increase can also have a growing global voice in theological education and in sharing the stories of what God is doing in Asia. This book has aimed to make a start in those endeavors.

God's Mission and Ours

We end where this book began – with God's mission to raise up a people for his glory, a people to demonstrate his character and share in his work. If he has chosen to use TEE as part of this great purpose, it is not because TEE is any kind of magic potion. It isn't. TEE has no power in itself to change lives. It is God who transforms by his Spirit. This book is intended to be a tribute to this great God by giving examples of what he is doing right across Asia today in and through his people.

SUGGESTED NEXT STEPS FOR YOU

Connect

- If you are interested in TEE in a particular country, get in touch using the contact details at the end of that chapter. Get to know the team and maybe visit them.

Pray

- Use the general prayer guidelines at the end of each chapter in part B.
- Ask to receive the short weekly prayer bulletin for Increase and its member bodies at increaseassociation@gmail.com.
- Some national TEE organizations produce their own prayer updates. See the contact information for some of them at the end of the chapters.

Help

Each national team may have specific needs, but here are some general ideas.

- You could serve short term if there is something useful to do. Or better, go long term, learn the language, and serve alongside a national team under national leadership.
- Many teams would appreciate help with English-language communications including newsletters and grant proposals that can raise awareness and support for their work. You could help in this area from your own country.
- You could help a team with your skills in websites, databases, audits, or other ways.
- The Increase Association itself also welcomes similar help.

Give

- Most national TEE programs are chronically underfunded despite being very cost effective. Better funding would open up many new possibilities.
- Give to a national team and help raise support, for example through a church link.
- Instead of going yourself, fund a local believer to become a TEE team member.
- You can also give to the work of Increase through the Increase Trust UK. Go to increaseassociation.org/donate/other-donors for details.

Try It

- Join a TEE group or attend a workshop to understand the method.
- Download sample lessons from SEAN at seaninternational.com/courses.html and try them out in group discussions in your church or prayer group.

Learn More

- There is much to explore on the Increase website: increaseassociation.org.
- Increase also plans to launch e-courses introducing TEE.
- See the online resource produced to help launch TEE discipleship groups at https://connect.crosswired.com/web/c2927223.

Stay Informed

- Increase is planning better communications through its website, Facebook, Twitter, and newsletters. Contact increaseassociation@gmail.com for more information.

Bibliography

Brown, Richard. "Theological Education by Extension in Central Asia: An Evaluation of Recent Trends and Future Trajectories through the Lens of the Religious Markets Theory." Unpublished paper, 2017.

Cooper, Alfredo. "Tools for Growth." unpublished paper, no date.

Graham, Billy. "What does it mean to be a disciple of Jesus?" *The Kansas City Star*, 15 May 2016. https://www.kansascity.com/living/liv-columns-blogs/billy-graham/article77272832.html.

Green, Douglas. "Labour migrants from Kyrgyzstan, Tajikistan and Uzbekistan to Russia Amidst Uncertain Trends," *Stratfor*, 6 September 2017. https://worldview.stratfor.com/article/labour-migrants-kyrgyzstan-tajikistan-and-uzbekistan-russia-amidst-uncertain-trends.

Green, Tim. "Should TEE in modern Asia be rejected, renewed or merely repackaged?" Unpublished paper, 2011.

Huggins, Michael. "The Open Russian Theological Academy." In *Diversified Theological Education: Equipping All God's People*, edited by Ross Kinsler, 269–95. Pasadena: William Carey International University, 2008.

Increase Association. "Diaspora Statement." https://www.increaseassociation.org/images/resources-library/diaspora-statement.pdf.

Kemp, Hugh. "Remembering Mongolia." Interserve. An excerpt from *GO Magazine*, 1 July 2015. https://interserve.org.au/story/199-remembering-mongolia/.

Kim, Joel. "Which Country Sends the [Second] Most Missionaries?" *Challies*, 21 February 2018. https://www.challies.com/articles/which-country-sends-the-second-most-missionaries/.

Kohl, Manfred Waldemar. "Theological Education: What Needs to be Changed?" *Torch Trinity Journal* 12 (2009): 149–62.

Lane, Joanne. "Sharing TEE in the Philippines." *GO Magazine* (July 2015): 22.

———. "Serving the Chinese Diaspora." *GO Magazine* (July 2015): 10.

Pulupe, Isaac. "Foreword." In *Christian Leaders' Training College Theological Education by Extension Prospectus*, revised July 2018.

SEAN International. "Je-Ju Vision Church: An excellent example of discipleship for rural and island churches," *SPREAD*, September 2010. https://www.seaninternational.com/news/SPREAD-SEPTEMBER-2010.pdf.

———. "Seoul Young Dong Church sets an excellent example of discipleship for metropolitan area churches." *SPREAD*, September 2010. https://www.seaninternational.com/news/SPREAD-SEPTEMBER-2010.pdf.

———. "South Korea," *SPREAD*, November 2016. https://www.seaninternational.com/news/november-2016/SPREAD-November-2016-English.pdf.

———. "Testimony from South Korea . . . 'Hello, my name is Jake Lim . . .'" *SPREAD*, April 2018. https://www.seaninternational.com/news/2018/04-18-SPREAD-Reduced.pdf.

Spycher, Ulrich, and Christina Spycher. *Singaut Magazine* 157 (Sept–Dec 2007): 1–15.

TEE Korea. "TEE Community Learning," 2013. https://www.teekorea.org:492/tong/uotc/uotc_view.asp?uotc_code=4203&uotc=19442&lef=01&sublef=undefined.

United Nations. "International Migration Report 2015 Highlights." New York: United Nations, 2016. https://www.un.org/en/development/desa/population/migration/publications/migrationreport/docs/MigrationReport2015_Highlights.pdf.

Vella, Jane. *Taking Learning to Task: Creative Strategies for Teaching Adults*. San Francisco: Jossey-Bass, 2001.

Webber, Malcolm. "Model Brief: Seven Key Paradigm Shifts." LeaderSource SGA, no date. https://www.leadersource.org/pdf/Core%20Model%20Brief%20Seven%20Key%20Paradigm%20Shifts.pdf.

Werner, Dietrich. *Challenges and Opportunities in Theological Education in the 21st Century: Pointers for a new international debate on Theological Education.* Edinburgh 2010: International study group on Theological Education World Study Report 2009. Joint Information Service of ETE & WOCATI, 2009. https://www.wocati.org/wp-content/uploads/2012/12/Challenges-and-Opportunities-in-Theological-Education-in-the-21st-Century-Prospects-for-a-New-International-Debate-on-Theological-Education.pdf.

Werner, Dietrich, and Namsoon Kang. "Theme 6 Theological Education and Formation." In *Mission Today and Tomorrow*, edited by Kirsteen Kim and Andrew Anderson, 158–165. Regnum Books International, 2011.

Weymouth, Rick J. "E-Learning and TEE: Our Future." Unpublished paper presented at the Increase conference "Empowering Churches, Equipping Disciples," Chiang Mai, Thailand, 16 November 2017.

Wright, Christopher J. H. *The Mission of God: Unlocking the Bible's Grand Narrative*. Downers Grove, IL: IVP Academic, 2006.

TEE for the
Twenty-First Century
A List of Recent Works

David Burke

Introduction

At first glance it may seem that the golden age of scholarly writing on TEE ended with the turn of the millennium. In 2004, Pat Harrison observed, "There appears to be an idea in some circles that TEE has had its day."[1] In 2011, Tim Green asked, "Has fresh thinking died in TEE?"[2]

Hold the obituary! A review of the literature suggests that Harrison was correct when she went on to say: "In fact, reports of the death of TEE have been greatly exaggerated."[3] TEE is alive and well at the level of scholarly literature as well as in a revitalized form and presence in the field.

The main bibliography below includes works on TEE published since 2000. Works with TEE or similar in the title have been included, along with some works known to include a significant discussion of TEE. Every effort has been made for comprehensiveness and accuracy both in inclusion and in citation details, although invariably there will be some gaps and errors. Apologies to those whose valuable writing was overlooked.

The materials listed below include newsletter items, press releases, case studies, theses and dissertations, journal articles, books, book chapters, online posts, and conference papers. They are published on a variety of platforms in

---

1. Patricia J. Harrison, "Forty Years On: The Evolution of Theological Education by Extension (TEE)," *Evangelical Review of Theology* 28, no. 4 (October 2004): 321.
2. Tim Green, "Should TEE in Modern Asia Be Rejected, Renewed or Merely Repackaged?" unpublished paper (2011), 3.
3. Harrison, "Forty Years On," 321.

diverse locations, which indicates the wide-ranging recognition of this form of ministry training as worthy of serious discussion.

But there was also a plethora of writing on TEE from 1970 to 2000. So a short list of representative works from some significant writers in this period is given first as a starting point for readers who are new to the field.

Representative Works Pre-2000

Harrison, Patricia J. "A Rural Australian Experiment in Training Church Leaders." *International Review of Mission* 71, no. 282 (April 1982): 184–192.

———. "Theological Education by Extension: A Progress Report." *Journal of Christian Education* 21, no. 1 (May 1978): 40–47.

Holland, Grace. *TEE Study Materials: Which Way for a Changing Africa?* Nairobi: Evangel Publishing, 1992; DMiss diss., Trinity Evangelical Divinity School, Chicago, 1992.

Kinsler, F. Ross. "Equipping God's People for Mission." *International Review of Mission* 71, no. 282 (April 1982): 133–144.

———. "Kairos in Theological Education: Changing Perspectives from the Underside." *British Journal of Theological Education* 2, no. 1 (1988): 1–13.

———, ed. *Ministry by the People: Theological Education by Extension*. New York: Orbis, 1983.

———. "Mission and Context: The Current Debate about Contextualization." *Evangelical Missions Quarterly* 14, no. 1 (January 1978): 23–29.

———. "Mission by the People." *International Review of Mission* 68, no. 271 (July 1979): 225–234.

———. "Theological Education by Extension: Service or Subversion?" *Missiology* 6, no. 2 (April 1978): 181–196.

———. "Theological Education by Extension Comes of Age: A Regional Survey." *International Review of Mission* 71, no. 282 (April 1982): 145–152.

Kinsler, F. Ross, and James H. Emery, ed. *Opting for Change: A Handbook on Evaluation and Planning for Theological Education by Extension*. Pasadena: William Carey, 1991.

Mulholland, Kenneth B. *Adventures in Training the Ministry: A Honduran Case Study in Theological Education by Extension*. Nutley: P&R Publishing, 1976.

———. "A Guatemalan Experiment Becomes a Model for Change." *International Review of Mission* 71, no. 282 (April 1982): 153–160.

————. "TEE Come of Age: A Candid Assessment after Two Decades." In *Cyprus: TEE Come of Age*, edited by Robert L. Youngblood, 9–25. Exeter: Paternoster, 1984.

Ward, Ted W. "Theological Education by Extension: Much More than a Fad." *Theological Education* 10, no. 4 (Summer 1974): 246–258.

————. "Types of TEE." *Evangelical Missions Quarterly* 13, no. 2 (April 1977): 74–85.

Ward, Ted W., and Margaret Ward. *Programmed Instruction for Theological Education by Extension*. East Lansing: Michigan State University Press, 1970; repr. 1971.

Ward, Ted W., and Samuel F. Rowen. "The Significance of the Extension Seminary." *Evangelical Missions Quarterly* 8, no. 4 (October 1972): 17–27.

Winter, Ralph D. *Theological Education by Extension*. South Pasadena: William Carey, 1969; reissued in 2008.

Works since 2000

Anderson, Justice C. *An Evangelical Saga: Baptists and Their Precursors in Latin America*. Longwood: Xulon, 2005.

————. "Theological Education by Extension." In *Evangelical Dictionary of World Missions*, edited by A. Scott Moreau, Harold Netland, and Charles Van Engen, 944. Grand Rapids: Baker, 2000.

Aylett, Graham P., ed. "Exploring New Horizons – Working Together for Church-Based Training in Asia." Proceedings of a conference held in Kuala Lumpur, Malaysia, 20–25 April 2015. Increase Association, 2015. https://www.increaseassociation.org/images/downloads/exploring-new-horizons.pdf.

————. "A Fresh Look at Theological Education by Extension." *ATA News*, July–September 2012.

Aylett, Graham, and Tim Green. "Theological Education by Extension (TEE) as a Tool for Twenty-First Century Mission." In *Reflecting on and Equipping for Christian Mission*, edited by Stephen Bevans, Teresa Chai, J. Nelson Jennings, Knud Jørgensen, and Dietrich Werner, 59–78. Regnum Edinburgh Centenary Series 27. Oxford: Regnum, 2015.

Baylor, Dave. "A Brief History of Theological Education by Extension." *For the Multitude*, 4 September 2009. http://web.archive.org/web/20100615184239/http://www.forthemultitude.org:80/2009/09/04/a-brief-history-of-theological-education-by-extension.

Bisset, Peter. "The Institute of TEE in Nepal." In *Diversified Theological Education: Equipping All God's People*, edited by F. Ross Kinsler, 107–132. William Carey International University Press, 2008.

Bontrager, Joseph. "Theological Education by Extension." *Global Anabaptist Mennonite Encyclopedia Online*, 30 June 2020. https://gameo.org/index.php?title=Theological_ Education_by_Extension&stableid=122808.

Brown, Richard. "Theological Education by Extension in Central Asia: An Evaluation of Recent Trends and Future Trajectories through the Lens of the Religious Markets Theory." Unpublished paper, 2018.

Burke, David. "TEE – The New Face in Ministry Training." *New Life* 81, no. 1 (1 July 2018): 12.

———. "Time to Leave the Wilderness? The Teaching of Pastoral Theology in South East Asia." In *Tending the Seedbeds: Educational Perspectives on Theological Education in Asia*, edited by Allan Harkness, 263–284. Quezon City: Asia Theological Association, 2010.

Burton, Sam W. *Disciple Mentoring: Theological Education by Extension.* Pasadena: William Carey, 2000.

Carey, Freda M. "Theological Education by Extension in Pakistan." *Ecumenical Review* 64, no. 2 (July 2012): 160–168.

Chatfield, Adrian. "The Question of Accreditation and Academic Standards in TEE." https://web.archive.org/web/20041204160340/http://teenet.net/ chatfieldaccreditation.htm.

Cheeseman, Graham. "Theological Education as Training." *TheologicalEducation.net*, 15 December 2011. http://theologicaleducation.net/articles/view.htm?id=113.

Cho, Stephen S. R. "Principles of Small Group Community Learning and Making Teaching Plans for Facilitators: A Study on the Effect of TEE Community Learning." ThD diss., BaikSuk Theological University, 2011.

Cho, Stephen S. R., and H. K. Jang. *Community Learning with TEE.* TEE Korea, 2012.

Davies, Sammy, Jr. "TEE (Theological Education by Extension)." *SaintBeagle*, April 2010. http://saintbeagle.wordpress.com/papers/tee-theological-education-by-extension.

Delamarter, Steve, and Daniel L. Brunner. "Theological Education and Hybrid Models of Distance Learning." *Theological Education* 40, no. 2 (2005): 145–164.

Dunn, Judith E. "What Is Wrong with the Preparation of Christian Workers in Colleges and Is Theological Education by Extension a Better Alternative?" theologicaleducation.org, 4 June 2010. http://theologicaleducationorg.files. wordpress.com/2010/06/essay-dunn.pdf.

Ekpunobi, Emmanuel. "Alternatives to Institutional Theological Education: A Proposal for Grass Root Theological Education." theologicaleducation.org, 20 September

2009. http://theologicaleducationorg.files.wordpress.com/2010/09/cte-02-alternatives-to-institutional-te.doc.

Elliott, John M. "Leadership Development and Relational Patterns: The Early Church and the Church in Zambia Today." DMin diss., Assemblies of God Theological Seminary, 2007. http://jd-elliott.net/Elliott_Leadership_Development_&_Relational_Patterns.pdf.

Evans, P. J. "What Is the Appropriate Form of Theological Education by Extension for Muslim Background Believers in One Central Asian Context and What Forms Need to Be Developed?" MA diss., University of Wales, 2012.

Gaikwad, Roger. "Theological Equipping of Ecclesia: An Asian Reflection on the Africa TEE Conference." *Ministerial Formation* 108 (January 2007): 25–29.

Glissmann, Volker. "Christian Reflective Practice: Prayer as a Tool for Reflection and Application in Theological Education." *InSights Journal* 2, no. 2 (2017): 35–52. https://insightsjournal.org/wp-content/uploads/2019/10/Christian-Reflective-Practice.pdf.

———. "The Fragmentation of Theological Education and Its Effect on the Church, TEE and Grassroots Theological Education in Malawi." In *Towards a Malawian Theology of Laity*, edited by Volker Glissmann. Mzuzu: Mzuzu University Press, 2019.

———. "The Role of Community in Theological Education by Extension (TEE)." *The Theological Educator*, 10 April 2015. https://thetheologicaleducator.net/2015/04/10/the-role-of-community-in-theological-education-by-extension-tee.

———. "What Is Theological Education by Extension?" *The Theological Educator*, 28 November 2014. https://thetheologicaleducator.net/2014/11/28/what-is-theological-education-by-extension.

Green, Tim. "Should TEE in Modern Asia Be Rejected, Renewed or Merely Repackaged?" Unpublished paper, 2011. Available from the author: tmwgreen@gmail.com.

Greig, E. "An Evaluation on SEAN Material as a Piece of Scripture Engagement." MA diss., Redcliffe College, 2016.

Harkness, Allan. "Seminary to Pew to Home, Workplace and Community – and Back Again: The Role of Theological Education in Asian Church Growth." Paper Presented at OMF International Consultation on Ecclesiology and Discipleship, Singapore, 2–5 April 2013. Available from the author: allan.harkness@gmail.com.

Harms, F. Hartwig. "Writing for T.E.E.: A Handbook for Training Authors." Unpublished paper, 2003. Available from the author: hartwig.harms@t-online.de.

Harrison, Patricia J. "Forty Years On: The Evolution of Theological Education by Extension (TEE)." *Evangelical Review of Theology* 28, no. 4 (October 2004): 315–328.

Hauser, Brian H. "A Theological Education by Extension Course on the Book of Psalms for Use in Côte d'Ivoire." MA diss., Emmanuel School of Religion, 2001.

Increase Association. "Exploring New Horizons Conference." Increase Association, 2015. https://www.increaseassociation.org/news-archive/exploring-new-horizons-conference-report.

———. "Increase Association Pan-Asia Conference 2017." Increase Association, 2017. https://www.increaseassociation.org/images/stories/Increase-Conference-Nov-2017-Press-Release.pdf.

———. "Kathmandu 2010 Conference Statement." Increase Association, 2010. https://www.increaseassociation.org/news-archive/31-kathmandu-2010-conference-statement.

———. "Kathmandu 2010 Press Release." Increase Association, 2010. https://www.increaseassociation.org/news-archive/32-kathmandu-2010-pressrelease.

Interserve England & Wales. "Building the Church: How Theological Education by Extension Helps Build the Church in Asia." *GO Magazine*, Jan–Mar 2011.

Joseph, Yakubu, and Sati Umaru Fwatshak. "Baseline Study of the Environmental Sustainability and Climate Change Program of the Theological Education by Extension (TEE) of the Ekklesiyar Yan'uwa a Nigeria (EYN): Report," Mission 21, January 2014. http://businessdocbox.com/Agriculture/69153662-Report-january-yakubu-joseph-university-of-tubingen-germany-prof-sati-umaru-fwatshak-university-of-jos-nigeria-disclaimer.html.

Kemp, Roger. "Towards Excellence in Theological Education?" *Evangelical Review of Theology* 28, no. 4 (October 2004): 329–336.

Kinsler, F. Ross. "Birth of a Movement: TEE." *Mission Frontiers* (May–Aug 2009): 24. http://www.missionfrontiers.org/pdfs/31-3-4-kinsler.pdf.

———, ed. *Diversified Theological Education: Equipping All God's People*. Pasadena: William Carey International University Press, 2008.

———. "Doing Ministry for a Change? Theological Education for the Twenty-First Century." *Ministerial Formation* 108 (January 2007): 4–13.

———. "Equipping All God's People for God's Mission." In *Diversified Theological Education: Equipping All God's People*, ed. F. Ross Kinsler, 15–32. Pasadena: William Carey International University Press, 2008.

———. "Relevance and Importance of TEF/PTE/ETE. Vignettes from the Past and Possibilities for the Future." *Ministerial Formation* 110 (April 2008): 10–17.

Kohl, Manfred W. "Current Trends in Theological Education." *International Congregational Journal* 1 (2001): 26–40.

———. "Radical Transformation in Preparation for the Ministry." *International Congregational Journal* 6, no. 1 (Fall 2006): 39–51.

Kriel, Pieter F. "Workers for the Harvest: Producing and Training Leaders the Church Needs to Fulfill Its Missionary Task." PhD diss., University of Pretoria, 2009. http://hdl.handle.net/2263/28180.

Kuligin, Victor. "Going the Distance: Adapting Full-time Residential Curricula into Distance Format." *Evangelical Missions Quarterly* 43, no. 3 (July 2007): 298–305.

Lo, James. "Seven Ingredients of Successful TEE Programs." *Evangelical Missions Quarterly* 38, no. 3 (July 2002): 338–341.

Mabuluki, Kangwa. "Diversified Theological Education: Genesis, Development and Ecumenical Potential of Theological Education by Extension (TEE)." In *Handbook of Theological Education in World Christianity. Theological Perspectives, Ecumenical Trends, Regional Surveys*, edited by Dietrich Werner, David Esterline, Namsoon Kang, and Joshva Raja, 251–62. Oxford: Regnum, 2010.

———. "The Relevance of TEE in African Training for Mission." In *Reflecting on and Equipping for Christian Mission*, edited by Stephen Bevans, Teresa Chai, J. Nelson Jennings, Knud Jørgensen, and Dietrich Werner, 79–89. Regnum Edinburgh Centenary Series 27. Oxford: Regnum, 2015.

———. "Theological Education for All God's People: Theological Education by Extension (TEE) in Africa." In *Handbook of Theological Education in Africa*, edited by Isabel Apawo Phiri and Dietrich Werner, 832–840. Oxford: Regnum, 2013.

Nkonge, Dickson K. "Theological Education Institutions in Kenya and the Future of the Church: An Anglican Case Study." *Journal of Adult Theological Education* 10, no. 2 (November 2013): 147–161.

Oriedo, Simon J. "The Theological Education by Extension (T.E.E.) Programme of the Anglican Church of Kenya: A Case Study." MEd diss., University of South Africa, 2010. http://hdl.handle.net/10500/3994.

Ott, Bernhard. *Understanding and Developing Theological Education*. Carlisle: Langham Global Library, 2016.

Ro, Bong Rin, Ken Gnanakan, and Joseph Shao, eds. *New Era, New Vision: Celebrating 40 Years of the Asia Theological Association*. Quezon City: Asia Theological Association, 2010.

Schafroth, Verena. "Theological Education by Extension in South Sudan." *Evangelical Review of Theology* 34, no. 2 (2010): 167–175.

Schirrmacher, Thomas. *An Appeal for Alternative Education Models for Church and Missions*. MBS Texte 14. Berlin: Martin Bucer Seminar, 2004. https://www.bucer. de/fileadmin/_migrated/tx_org/mbstexte014.pdf.

———. "Special Address." Presented at the Increase 2010 Pan-Asia TEE conference, "Twenty-First Century TEE in Asia: Challenges and Opportunities." Kathmandu, Nepal, October 2010. https://www.increaseassociation.org/news-archive/35-dr-thomas-schirrmacher-s-addressin-kathmandu-october-2010.

SEAN International. "About SEAN International: How to Best Use SEAN Courses." http://www.seaninternational.com/best_use.html.

———. "Day of Prayer Celebration and Challenge: 14 of July 2014." http://www.seaninternational.com/news/2014_SEAN_DAY_OF_PRAYER_07-EN-5.pdf.

———. "SEAN 1971 to 2011!!" *SPREAD Newsletter* (August 2011): 2. http://www.seaninternational.com/news/SPREAD_AUGUST_2011_final.pdf.

Sendegeya, Fareth, and Leon Spencer. *Understanding TEE: A Course Outline and Handbook for Students and Tutors in Residential Theological Institutions in Africa*. Dar Es Salaam: ANITEPAM, 2001.

Shiferaw, Sadii. "Input on the Role of Theological Education by Extension – Decentering Education." Paper presented at the 4th All Africa Theological Education by Extension Conference, Addis Ababa, Ethiopia, 12–16 October 2014.

———. "Theological Education by Extension in the Ethiopian Evangelical Church Mekane Yesus: Towards Relevant Programmes." DTh diss., University of Birmingham, 2003.

Sills, Michael D. "Training Leaders for the Majority World Church in the 21st Century." *Global Missiology* 3, no. 1 (April 2004). http://ojs.globalmissiology.org/index.php/english/article/viewFile/130/377.

Smith, Richard. "To Evaluate Participants' Perceptions of the Value of Selected Aspects of Theological Education by Extension's Educational Methodology and Curriculum as Effective Preparation for a Selected Range of Christian Ministries in Bangladesh." MTh diss., Laidlaw-Carey Graduate School of Theology, 2009.

Smith, Rick, and Mary E. Snodderly. "Missiological Education by Extension: A Case Study of the Course 'Foundations of the World Christian Movement.'" *Christian Perspectives in Education* 4, no. 1 (2010).

Stauss, Wolfgang. "TEE (Theological Education by Extension) – What Works and What Doesn't?" Unpublished paper, 2012.

Steyn, Gert J. "The Future of Theological Education by Extension (TEE) in Africa." *Missionalia* 32, no. 1 (April 2004): 3–22.

Taylor, Michael, and Craig Dunsmuir. "Theological Education by Extension: A Case Study on TEE College Johannesburg." In *Handbook of Theological Education in Africa*, edited by Isabel Apawo Phiri and Dietrich Werner, 958–965. Oxford: Regnum, 2013.

Völker, Markus. "Successfully Completing a TEE Programme: An Analysis of Factors Which Assist TEE students in the IEP Arequipa Region (Peru) to Study Successfully in Spite of High Dropout Rates." DMin diss., Columbia International University, European School of Culture and Theology, 2016.

Vysotskaya, Anneta. "Een nieuwe generatie kerkelijk werkers: De kracht van Theological Education by Extension in voormalige Sovjet-landen." *TussenRuimte* 8, no. 4 (2015): 48–53.

———. "De situatie van christenen in Centraal-Azië wordt steeds slechter." *Alle Volken* 105, no. 1 (2012): 4–5.

———. "Theological Education in the Context of Persecution and Economic Hardship: Focus on TEE in Central Asia." *International Journal for Religious Freedom* 5, no. 2 (2012): 111–122.

Wahl, Willem P. "Theological Education in an African Context: Discipleship and Mediated Learning Experience as Framework." PhD diss., University of the Free State, 2011. http://hdl.handle.net/11660/2100.

Ward, Ted. "Theological Education by Extension." In *Evangelical Dictionary of Christian Education*, edited by Michael J. Anthony, 692–693. Grand Rapids: Baker Academic, 2001.

Ward, Ted W., and Samuel F. Rowen. "The Rail-Fence Analogy for the Education of Leaders." *Common Ground Journal* 11, no. 1 (Fall 2013): 47–51.

Waugh, Geoff. *The Body of Christ, Part 2: Ministry Education*. Charleston: CreateSpace, 2010.

Weymouth, Rick J. "E-Learning and TEE: Our Future." Paper presented at the Increase conference "Empowering Churches, Equipping Disciples," Chiang Mai, Thailand, 16 November 2017.

———. "Four Short Articles on E-Learning and TEE in One Document." 2017. This document contains: "E-Learning and TEE: An Introductory Paper," 2010; "Issues to Consider as You Move Forward in E-Learning," 2010; "Issues to Consider as You Move Forward in E-Learning," 2017; "Relationality in E-Learning for PTEE," 2009.

———. "The Shape of E-Learning in the PTEE." Report presented at the 30th Annual Meeting of the PTEE, Amman, Jordan, 2011.

Wilson, Karen M. "Contextualized Bible Study and Theological Education in Meru Society: Liberation Theology Principles in the Development Context of East Africa." MA diss., University of Manchester, 2008.

Winter, Ralph, and William Jeynes. "Theological Education by Extension and Protestant Education in Guatemala." In *International Handbook of Protestant Education*, edited by William Jeynes and David W. Robinson, 373–387. International Handbooks of Religion and Education 6. Dordrecht: Springer, 2012.

———. "Theological Education by Extension and the Significance of the Armenia, Columbia Meeting." In *International Handbook of Protestant Education*, edited by William Jeynes and David W. Robinson, 389–398. International Handbooks of Religion and Education 6. Dordrecht: Springer, 2012.

The Editors and Authors

Dr Graham Aylett
Graham is an Interserve partner and served with the national TEE program in Mongolia for fourteen years. He now works as part of the Increase support team with Tim Green from a base in England. Graham is vice-chair of the trustees of SEAN International and on the Commission for Accreditation and Educational Development of the Asia Theological Association (ATA).

Dr David Ball
David was born in Kenya where his parents were missionaries. David and his wife spent almost fifteen years in India working with TAFTEE before returning to the UK where he now works part time as a consultant for SEAN International and part time as Director of the GOLD Project.

Claire Boxall
Claire lives and works in southeast England and has a background in public relations and communications for not for profit organizations. She currently juggles strategic development and strategic communications roles for three organizations and volunteers with youth and international development charities, as well as in her local Methodist church.

David Burke
David is an Australian pastor and teacher who spent twelve years ministering in Singapore. He presently teaches at Christ College in Sydney and is increasingly involved in various forms of ministry training in Asia.

Dr Tim Green
An Interserve partner since 1988, Tim served with the national TEE programs in Pakistan and Jordan. He works as Increase general secretary and is a trustee of SEAN International. Tim has written two SEAN courses and other courses using audio-visual media. He presently lives in Southeast Asia and is a special consultant to the World Evangelical Association (WEA) in church-based training.

ML Low

ML, a keen photographer and author of a book, had her early career in the capital markets. She served the Lord as editor of her church magazine for ten years while she was a homemaker.

Bob Teoh

Bob and his wife, Kim, are bi-vocational missionaries with World Outreach International serving in Southeast Asia and were based in Malaysia before recently relocating to Australia. Bob is also a journalist.

Dr Penelope Vinden

Penny was brought up in Canada and taught cross-cultural psychology at a university in the USA. She then moved to England and worked with the communications team of the International Fellowship of Evangelical Students (IFES) for nine years before becoming a freelance writer.

Hanna-Ruth van Wingerden

Hanna-Ruth studied history but went on to train as an English teacher. She and her husband served with the GZB, a Dutch mission agency and partner of Increase, in Central Asia for four years. Now living in the Netherlands, she teaches English and Dutch, serves in the Central Asia Vision Group, and works for Increase part time.

ICETE

International Council for Evangelical Theological Education
strengthening evangelical theological education through International cooperation

ICETE is a global community, sponsored by nine regional networks of theological schools, to enable international interaction and collaboration among all those engaged in strengthening and developing evangelical theological education and Christian leadership development worldwide.

The purpose of ICETE is:
1. To promote the enhancement of evangelical theological education worldwide.
2. To serve as a forum for interaction, partnership and collaboration among those involved in evangelical theological education and leadership development, for mutual assistance, stimulation and enrichment.
3. To provide networking and support services for regional associations of evangelical theological schools worldwide.
4. To facilitate among these bodies the advancement of their services to evangelical theological education within their regions.

Sponsoring associations include:

Africa: Association for Christian Theological Education in Africa (ACTEA)

Asia: Asia Theological Association (ATA)

Caribbean: Caribbean Evangelical Theological Association (CETA)

Europe: European Evangelical Accrediting Association (EEAA)

Euro-Asia: Euro-Asian Accrediting Association (E-AAA)

Latin America: Association for Evangelical Theological Education in Latin America (AETAL)

Middle East and North Africa: Middle East Association for Theological Education (MEATE)

North America: Association for Biblical Higher Education (ABHE)

South Pacific: South Pacific Association of Evangelical Colleges (SPAEC)

www.icete-edu.org

Langham Literature and its imprints are a ministry of Langham Partnership.

Langham Partnership is a global fellowship working in pursuit of the vision God entrusted to its founder John Stott –

> *to facilitate the growth of the church in maturity and Christ-likeness through raising the standards of biblical preaching and teaching.*

Our vision is to see churches in the Majority World equipped for mission and growing to maturity in Christ through the ministry of pastors and leaders who believe, teach and live by the word of God.

Our mission is to strengthen the ministry of the word of God through:
* nurturing national movements for biblical preaching
* fostering the creation and distribution of evangelical literature
* enhancing evangelical theological education

especially in countries where churches are under-resourced.

Our ministry

Langham Preaching partners with national leaders to nurture indigenous biblical preaching movements for pastors and lay preachers all around the world. With the support of a team of trainers from many countries, a multi-level programme of seminars provides practical training, and is followed by a programme for training local facilitators. Local preachers' groups and national and regional networks ensure continuity and ongoing development, seeking to build vigorous movements committed to Bible exposition.

Langham Literature provides Majority World preachers, scholars and seminary libraries with evangelical books and electronic resources through publishing and distribution, grants and discounts. The programme also fosters the creation of indigenous evangelical books in many languages, through writer's grants, strengthening local evangelical publishing houses, and investment in major regional literature projects, such as one volume Bible commentaries like *The Africa Bible Commentary* and *The South Asia Bible Commentary*.

Langham Scholars provides financial support for evangelical doctoral students from the Majority World so that, when they return home, they may train pastors and other Christian leaders with sound, biblical and theological teaching. This programme equips those who equip others. Langham Scholars also works in partnership with Majority World seminaries in strengthening evangelical theological education. A growing number of Langham Scholars study in high quality doctoral programmes in the Majority World itself. As well as teaching the next generation of pastors, graduated Langham Scholars exercise significant influence through their writing and leadership.

To learn more about Langham Partnership and the work we do visit **langham.org**

CPSIA information can be obtained
at www.ICGtesting.com
Printed in the USA
BVHW071048110321
602311BV00002B/62

9 781839 730658